ISBN 978-1-331-44147-2
PIBN 10190686

English
Français
Deutsche
Italiano
Español
Português

www.forgottenbooks.com

Mythology Photography **Fiction**
Fishing Christianity **Art** Cooking
Essays Buddhism Freemasonry
Medicine **Biology** Music **Ancient**
Egypt Evolution Carpentry Physics
Dance Geology **Mathematics** Fitness
Shakespeare **Folklore** Yoga Marketing
Confidence Immortality Biographies
Poetry **Psychology** Witchcraft
Electronics Chemistry History **Law**
Accounting **Philosophy** Anthropology
Alchemy Drama Quantum Mechanics
Atheism Sexual Health **Ancient History**
Entrepreneurship Languages Sport
Paleontology Needlework Islam
Metaphysics Investment Archaeology
Parenting Statistics Criminology
Motivational

S205V

95¢

Christ and Adam

Man and Humanity in Romans 5

Karl Barth

With an Introduction by **Wilhelm Pauck**

hrist and Adam

AND HUMANITY IN ROMANS 5

KARL BARTH

CHRIST

AND ADAM

Man and Humanity in Romans 5

Translated by T. A. SMAIL

COLLIER BOOKS
NEW YORK, N.Y.

This Collier Books edition is published
by arrangement with Harper & Brothers

Collier Books is a division of The Crowell-
Collier Publishing Company

First Collier Books Edition 1962

This work is a translation of Karl Barth's *Christus und Adam
nach Römer 5* published in 1952 by the Evangelischer Verlag
in Zollikon-Zurich

Hecho en los E.E.U.U.
Printed in the United States of America

INTRODUCTION

WILHELM PAUCK

The fifth chapter of the Epistle to the Romans, on which Barth here fixes his attention, has been of special importance in the history of Christian thought. It was largely through the influence of Augustine that certain of Paul's ideas expressed in this part of his most powerful letter came to play a major role in the theology of Roman Catholicism and in that of the Protestant Reformation. Romans 5:5—"the love of God is shed abroad in our hearts by the Holy Spirit"—furnished the Scriptural basis for the theology of grace and the sacraments, chiefly in relation to the word *ekkechutai* which in later versions is translated by "is shed abroad" but was rendered in the Vulgate by *infusa est* ("was infused").

Furthermore, Romans 5:12—"As sin came into the world through one man and death through sin, and so death spread to all men because all men

7

sinned"—became the Scriptural keystone of the doctrine of original sin. The teaching that Adam's sin and its penalty (death) is passed on to all men was explained by way of an exegesis of these words, especially in connection with the fact that the phrase "for that" *(eph'hō),* meaning "because," appeared in the Vulgate translation as *"in quo"* ("in whom"). Hence the words of the Apostle were understood to mean that, in view of the fact that all men sin in Adam, sin and death entered the world through him. On the basis of this teaching, the Pauline conception of the two humanities, one headed by Adam and the other by Christ (Rom. 5:12-21), then assumed special significance in relation to the doctrine of the atonement.

In this essay, Barth does not deal with all these doctrines. His interest is concentrated upon the relation between Christ and Adam as the Apostle understood it. By-passing the entire exegetical and theological tradition built upon this chapter of the Pauline Epistle, Barth offers an entirely new and unprecedented interpretation of the conception of man implied in the Apostle's view of the relation between Christ and Adam.

The treatise must then be read in the light of three considerations:

Introduction

(1) It is a contribution to the interpretation of the famed fifth chapter of Paul's Epistle to the Romans. (2) It is an example of Barth's distinctive exegetical method. (3) It illumines the significance of a theme that is central in Barth's crowning systematic achievement, the *Church Dogmatics*.[1]

Let us briefly deal with these three topics:

(1) The fifth chapter of the Epistle to the Romans presents special difficulties to the exegete not only because of the intricate reasoning of its author, the Apostle Paul, but chiefly on account of the parallel between Adam and Christ which Paul introduces in connection with his argument about the universal sinfulness of men, both Jews and Gentiles. The curse of sin, he says, cannot be undone by human works of the law but only through divine justification that must be received in faith.

---

[1] This work, begun in 1931, is designed to consist of five volumes: I. *The Doctrine of the Word of God.* II. *The Doctrine of God.* III. *The Doctrine of Creation.* IV. *The Doctrine of Reconciliation.* V. *The Doctrine of Redemption.* To date, these volumes have been published in several parts: I, 1 and 2; II, 1 and 2; III, 1-4; IV, 1 and 2. Other parts of IV and V are in preparation. A group of Scottish theologians is now engaged in the task of translating the entire work. To date, editions in English have been published in 1956 and 1957 respectively, of I, 1 and 2, and IV, 1, by Charles Scribner's Sons, New York. Otto Weber has provided an "introductory report" on I, 1 to III, 4; see *Karl Barth's Church Dogmatics* (Philadelphia: Westminster Press, 1954).

Introduction

The reasoning of the Apostle, always subtle, is particularly difficult to follow in this passage, especially in the second part of the chapter, vv. 12-21. Here Adam is pictured as the "type of him who is to come." He by whom sin, and consequently death, entered into the world is seen as the one who prefigures the Redeemer through whose death and resurrection all mankind is saved. The Apostle thus appears to think of two heads of humanity: Adam, by whose disobedience many were made sinners, and Christ, by whose obedience many are to be made righteous (Rom. 5:19). Indeed, Adam is viewed as the head of sinful mankind that is doomed to die and Christ as the head of a new humanity that has the promise of eternal life.

In the course of Christian history, Barth implies, these ideas linking men's predicament of sin with Adam, the first man, and their hope of freedom from sin with Christ, came to receive a stress far removed from the intention and meaning of Paul: Adam, as the father of the race, was viewed as the originator of sin. In dependence upon him, through the sexual connection of one generation with another, all mankind became a "mass of perdition," to recall Augustine's words. By heredity, men were supposed to be inescapably caught up in "original sin"; the "sin of the origin" was felt to taint all its members. Only those who "put on the Lord Jesus Christ" could hope to be liberated from the "curse of Adam." Thus this particular Pauline passage became the basis of one of the most powerful and influential doctrines in the history of Christendom: the union of all men in Adam, the first sinner, in whom they all find their condemnation.

Although surprisingly Barth makes no direct reference to this historic teaching, he evidently has it in mind throughout his commentary. Barth's prime purpose is to correct this age-old tradition by pointing out that Paul is not correctly understood unless one recognizes that the Apostle sees Christ as the true head of *all* humanity, Adam included—the triumphant head of that humanity which, beginning with Adam's transgression, is doomed to death, because all its members have sinned and do sin like Adam.

(2) The method of exegesis which Barth employs in the present essay has the same flavor and cast as the many exegetical essays which it has been his custom to include in his large dogmatic work. He tries to think through closely the meanings and affirmations of the Biblical text. His one purpose is to make plain what the Biblical authors wanted to say. He

therefore pays strict attention to the context of the passage he has to expound, taking every word with utmost seriousness. Persuaded that the message of the Bible constitutes a unity, he carefully tries to bring the whole Bible to bear upon each of its parts. He does not choose to interpret the Bible historically, though he does not hesitate to use historical insights about the origin and the original purpose of the individual Biblical works.

In this essay, he concentrates his attention almost entirely upon the passage at hand. Only occasionally does he glance at other books of the Bible (e.g., 1 Cor. 15:21-22; 45-49, where Paul also relates Adam and Christ to each other). He does not refer to other commentators (although it is apparent that he is mindful of the work of some of them). He refrains entirely from an inquiry into the sources of Paul's ideas, terms, and forms of speech. Nor does he compare the teachings of the Apostle with those of his contemporaries and his predecessors and followers. He therefore does not seem to attribute any significance to the evidence that it is in Jewish Rabbinic literature that one finds for the first time the story of Adam's fall so interpreted as to explain the origin of the fact that all men sin. Nor does Barth display any interest in the evidence purporting to prove that the idea of the connection between the sin and death of Adam and that of his descendants was first advanced in such writings as the *Wisdom of Solomon* and the *Books of Enoch*.[2] Moreover, he pays no attention to the question of how Paul's conception of Christ as the second Adam may be related to similar ideas of his contemporary Philo, the Alexandrian Jewish philosopher, or how it is to be understood in the light of the early Christian interpretation of Jesus as the "Son of Man," etc.[3]

We must assume that Barth does not take account of such problems because he is not concerned to interpret the Epistle to the Romans in the manner of historical exegesis. For him the Epistle is first and foremost part of the canon of the New Testament to which, according to his view, Christian theology must orient itself as to the Word of God.

(3) There is a close relation between the thesis of this exegetical treatise and one of the basic themes of Barth's *Church Dogmatics*. This grand work is conceived as a theology of God's Word, that is, theology that deals with God's revelation in Jesus Christ

[2] N. P. Williams, *The Ideas of the Fall and of Original Sin* (2nd ed. New York: Longmans, Green and Co., 1929).
[3] Cf., e.g. Elias Andrews, *The Meaning of Christ for Paul* (Nashville and New York: Abingdon Press, 1949), pp. 93 ff.

13

as it is attested in the Bible. In method and basic theme, the *Dogmatics* is set in opposition to every brand of natural theology whether found in Roman Catholic Thomism or modern Protestantism: Barth's *magnum opus* does not proceed from man's knowledge of God and does not undertake to explain the meaning of the Christian gospel in the light of *man's religion:* it avows itself an exposition of God's disclosure of himself in Jesus Christ and of all that is implied therein for the understanding of man and his cosmos. Barth, therefore, does not move upwards from man to God, but downwards from God, or rather Christ, to man, and he erects his theology on the doctrinal foundations of the Word of God, the Trinity and the Incarnation.

It is a system of thought intended to be Biblical through and through. In the course of time, it has become more and more Christological: The man Christ Jesus is the key to the understanding of creation, reconciliation and redemption, and of the nature and destiny of man.

Barth has never deviated from the course he thus set for himself. Hence he has not hesitated to forsake time-honored modes of theological thought rather than modify his basic principle in any way; in all respects, insists Barth, Jesus Christ, the Son of God made Man, and only He is the "light in which we see light" (Ps. 36.9). Finding himself compelled by the Biblical witness to ground all doctrines in Christology, he develops the doctrine of creation on the basis of soteriology (*Church Dogmatics* III, 1) and he radically rethinks the doctrine of predestination by focusing its meaning on the person of Christ (III, 2). In the same way, he constructs the doctrine of man: human nature must be understood in the light of the nature of Christ. Adam and all his descendants, that is, all human history, its beginnings and its endings, its fallings and risings, its sin and its redemption, must be seen under the aspect of Jesus Christ in whom God became Man, that is, in whom God has declared himself incontrovertibly, unchangeably for man.

We must realize that this Christological view of man implies a radical departure from all ordinary general doctrines of man, including the traditional theological "anthropologies."

According to Barth, man and mankind must not be interpreted in terms of Adam, that is, in the light of biological or historical or philosophical conceptions of human nature. Rather, the only indispensable precondition for an understanding of human nature is the fact of God's revelation of Himself in the man Jesus. Nor dare we regard Jesus himself as the "perfect" or "ideal" man and as such one of the children of Adam, nor as the head of a new humanity that follows upon or supersedes the race begun by Adam. He who is "the revealing word of God, is the source of our knowledge of the human nature God has made." (III, 2, p. 47.)

It is still more important that Barth's doctrine of man involves also a reinterpretation of traditional theological anthropology. He agrees that the condemnation lying upon mankind because of sin (that of Adam, the first one of the race, and that of every other man) is real. Its gloom and doom may not be minimized. But because there is a higher order of humanity than that of Adam, an order disclosed in God's election of man in Christ, the burden of man's sin, guilt and death can never be the first or primary word about man's nature and destiny nor the key to the understanding of them. For, because in Christ God has become Man and because God has chosen Man in Christ, human nature and human life must be seen as resting upon a foundation that can never be shaken. The destiny of man is grounded upon the promise of God and no human defiance of the ends for which the world was created, can undo it.

The reader of the following essay should keep

these teachings of Barth in mind. He will find them extensively treated in Vol. IH, 2 of the *Church Dogmatics*, whose 800 pages constitute but a single chapter, entitled "The Creature."

Barth again directs his attention to anthropology in Vol. IV, 1, which has recently appeared in translation. He devotes part of a chapter entitled "Jesus Christ, the Lord as Servant" to a discussion of "The Pride and Fall of Man." Here he makes specific use of the teachings of Romans 5. What he has to say is closely paralleled by the exegesis offered in this little essay. A summary of his exposition may prove helpful. Thus he writes:

When the word "all" is used (in Romans 5:12), it is very much to the point to think of what we mean by the word "history." The verdict that all have sinned certainly implies a verdict on that which is human history apart from the will and word and work of God . . . and a knowledge of the sin and guilt of man in the light of the word of grace of God implies a knowledge that this history is, in fact, grounded and determined by the pride of man [p. 505]. . . . History is concluded in disobedience. This does not mean that it is outside of divine control. . . . The history of the world which God made in Jesus Christ, and with a view to him, cannot cease to have its center and goal in him. But in the light of this goal and center God cannot say Yes but only No to its corruption [p. 506]. . . .

What is the obviously outstanding feature of world history? . . . [It] is the all-conquering monotony—the monotony of the pride in which man has obviously always lived to his own detriment and that of his neighbor, from hoary antiquity and through the ebb and flow of his later progress and recession both as a whole and in detail, the pride in which he still lives . . . and will most certainly continue to do so till the end of time.

The Bible gives to this history and to all men in this sense the general title of Adam [p. 507]. . . . The name of Adam the transgressor sums up this history as the history of mankind which God has given up, given up to its pride on account of its pride . . . and . . . this is the explanation of its staggering monotony, this is the reason why there never can be any progress—it continually corresponds to his history. . . . It constantly re-enacts the little scene in the Garden of Eden. There never was a golden age. There is no point in looking back to one. The first man was immediately the first sinner [p. 508].

Who is Adam? . . . He was in a trivial form what we all are, a man of sin. But he was so as the beginner, and therefore as *primus inter pares* (first among equals). This does not mean that he has bequeathed to us as his heirs so that we have to be as he was. He has not poisoned us or passed on a disease. What we do after him is not done according to an example which irresistibly overthrows us, or an imitation of his act which is or-

18

dained for all his successors. No one has to be Adam. We are so freely and on our own responsibility [p. 509]. ... We and he are reached by the same Word and judgment of God in the same direct way [p. 510]. ...

What is Adam to Paul? What is to him the relevant thing in this primitive representative of humanity ... ? The fact that according to Rom. 5:12, he is the one man by whom "sin entered into the world and death by sin; and so that death passed upon all men because all have sinned." ... But how does he know it? ... Where has he found this? ... In Gen. 3, of course. But how could Gen. 3 become to him, as it obviously is, the divine Word which is decisive and normative and authoritative for his whole understanding of mankind and the history of man?

According to the text of Rom. 5:12-21 there is only one answer to this question. In that first and isolated figure ... in that great and typical sinner and debtor at the head of the whole race, in that dark representative of all his successors that bear his name, he recognized quite a different figure. This other, too, came directly from God, not as a creature only, but as the Son of God and himself God by nature. He, too, was a sinner and debtor, but as the sinless and guiltless bearer of the sin of others, the sins of other men. He, too, is the representative of all others. ... He was not the *primus inter pares* in a sequence. He represented them as a genuine leader, making atonement by his obedience, covering their disobedience, justifying them before God (Rom. 5:18, 19).

Introduction

This Pauline argument is usually called the parallel between Adam and Christ. But at the very least we ought to speak of the parallel between Christ and Adam [p. 512]. . . . For [Paul] knew Jesus Christ first and then Adam. . . . In the unrighteous man at the head of the old race he saw again the righteous man at the head of the new. . . . The former is like the rainbow in relation to the sun. It is only a reflection of it. It has no independent existence. It cannot stand against it. It does not balance it. When weighted in the scales it is only like a feather. . . . Is it not clear who and what is the *primus* [first] and who and what the *posterius* [later]? Even when we are told in 1 Cor. 15:45 that Jesus Christ is the *eschatos Adam* [the last Adam] this does not mean that in relation to the first Adam of Gen. 3 he is the second, but rather that he is the first and true Adam of which the other is only a type . . . [p. 513].[4]

Such is Barth's view of man and humanity and of Adam and Christ.

In a brief Introduction, it is hardly proper to offer criticisms and evaluations of the work that is to follow. The reader must, therefore, judge for himself whether Barth has rightly read and understood what Paul wrote to the Romans and whether he has drawn the right conclusions for a true interpretation of the Christian faith.

[4] From *The Doctrine of Reconciliation*, Pt. I, Vol. IV of *Church Dogmatics* by Karl Barth. Reprinted with the permission of Charles Scribner's Sons.

ROMANS 5:12-21

[Greek transliteration from Nestle text.]

[12] Dia touto hōsper di' henos anthrōpou hē hamartia eis ton kosmon eisēlthen, kai dia tēs hamartias ho thanatos, kai houtōs eis pantas anthrōpous ho thanatos diēlthen, eph' hō pantes hēmarton: [13] achri gar nomou hamartia ēn en kosmō, hamartia de ouk ellogeitai mē ontos nomou; [14] alla ebasileusen ho thanatos apo Adam mechri Mōuseōs kai epi tous mē hamartēsantas epi tō homoiōmati tēs parabaseōs Adam, hos estin typos tou mellontos.

[15] All' oukh hōs to paraptōma, houtōs to charisma; ei gar tō tou henos paraptōmati hoi polloi apethanon, pollō mallon hē charis tou Theou kai hē dōrea en chariti tē tou henos anthrōpou Iēsou Christou eis tous pollous eperisseusen. [16] Kai oukh hōs di' henos hamartēsantos to dōrēma; to men gar krima ex henos eis katakrima, to de charisma ek pollōn paraptōmatōn eis dikaiōma. [17] Ei gar tō tou henos paraptōmati ho thanatos ebasileusen dia tou henos, pollō mallon hoi tēn perisseian tēs charitos kai tēs dōreas tēs dikaiosunēs lambanontes en zōē basileusousin dia tou henos Iēsou Christou.

[18] Ara oun hōs di' henos paraptōmatos eis pantas anthrōpous eis katakrima, houtōs kai di' henos dikaiō-

ROMANS 5:12-21

[English translation from the Revised Standard Version.]

¹² Therefore as sin came into the world through one man and death through sin, and so death spread to all men because all men sinned— ¹³ sin indeed was in the world before the law was given, but sin is not counted where there is no law. ¹⁴ Yet death reigned from Adam to Moses, even over those whose sins were not like the transgression of Adam, who was a type of the one who was to come.

¹⁵ But the free gift is not like the trespass. For if many died through one man's trespass, much more have the grace of God and the free gift in the grace of that one man Jesus Christ abounded for many. ¹⁶ And the free gift is not like the effect of that one man's sin. For the judgment following one trespass brought condemnation, but the free gift following many trespasses brings justification. ¹⁷ If, because of one man's trespass, death reigned through that one man, much more will those who receive the abundance of grace and the free gift of righteousness reign in life through the one man Jesus Christ.

¹⁸ Then as one man's trespass led to condemnation for all men, so one man's act of righteousness leads to

matos eis pantas anthrōpous eis dikaiōsin zōēs; [19] hōsper gar dia tēs parakoēs tou henos anthrōpou hamartōloi katestathēsan hoi polloi, houtōs kai dia tēs hypakoēs tou henos dikaioi katastathēsontai hoi polloi. [20] Nomos de pareisēlthen hina pleonasē to paraptōma; hou de epleonasen hē hamartia, hypereperisseusen hē charis, [21] hina hōsper ebasileusen hē hamartia en tō thanatō, houtōs kai hē charis basileusē dia dikaiosunēs eis zōēn aiōnion dia Iēsou Christou tou kuriou hēmōn.

acquittal and life for all men. [19] For as by one man's disobedience many were made sinners, so by one man's obedience many will be made righteous. [20] Law came in, to increase the trespass; but where sin increased, grace abounded all the more, [21] so that, as sin reigned in death, grace also might reign through righteousness to eternal life through Jesus Christ our Lord.

CHRIST AND ADAM:

MAN AND HUMANITY IN ROMANS 5

Romans 5:12-21, along with the first eleven verses of the chapter, is the first of a series of passages in which Paul develops the main theme of the first part of the epistle, as it is stated in the key verses Rom. 1:16-17. There it is made clear that the gospel is the revelation of *dikaiosunē* (righteousness)[1] also called *dikaiōsis* (justification; acquittal [Rom. 4:25 and 5:18]) and *dikaiōma* (righteous decision [Rom. 5:16])—i.e., the revelation of the final righteous decision of God, which, for everyone who acknowledges it in faith, is the power of God unto salvation —*dynamis Theou eis sōtērian*. Paul brings out the full implications of that statement in chapters 5-8, in each of which, though the context is different, the theme and the way it is treated are the same.

[1] Greek words appearing in the original text have been transliterated. Translations have been added in parentheses where helpful for comprehension.—Ed.

Christ and Adam

The basis of the detailed arguments of chapter 5 is laid down as follows in vv. 1-11: when this righteous decision of God becomes known to us and effective for us through our acknowledgment and grasp of it in faith (*dikaiōthentes ek pisteōs*, justified by faith), we have peace with God (v. 1), our struggle against Him has reached its limit and so can go no farther, the lordship of sin over us is broken. The same thing is expressed in v. 10, "we are now reconciled with God"; in v. 11, "we have now received reconciliation"; and in v. 21 where we are told that every alien lordship has now become for us a thing of the past. The clearest description of how this righteous decision of God has been effected is in v. 5, according to which the love of God Himself, His love toward us, has been poured forth into our hearts. That this has happened is the presupposition of our future salvation before the judgment of wrath (vv. 9-10); and, on its positive side, and in relation to the present, it is the presupposition of our hope of partaking in God's glory, of which (according to 3:23) we must, as sinners, have completely and finally fallen short. That is what has happened wherever God's righteous decision has been acknowledged and grasped in faith. That is why this righteous decision and the gospel that reveals it are called (1:16) "God's saving power." That is why we glory in such hope (v. 2). It will not let us be put to shame (v. 5). For, on this presupposition, even in our present afflictions we can only glory, because they can only make us the more steadfast, can only provide us with assurance, can, in this indirect way, serve only to summon us all the more to hope (vv. 3-4). God's righteous decision has such power to make peace with God for believers, to reconcile them to God, to pour forth God's love into their hearts, because it has been carried out in Jesus Christ, who is, quite uniquely (v. 7), the way by which we gain access to the grace in which (v. 2) we have taken our stand. For God's love toward us commends itself in this (v. 8), that Christ died for us while we were still weak (v. 6), still sinners (v. 8), still godless (v. 6), still enemies (v. 10). It has therefore not waited for us, but has come to meet us and gone before us. In sovereign anticipation of our faith God has justified us through the sacrificial blood of Christ. In the death of His Son God has intervened on our behalf in the "nevertheless" of His free grace in face of the apparently insurmountable power of our revolt and resistance (vv. 9-10). So He has made peace, so reconciled us, so commended His love toward us. Because God in Jesus Christ so exercises

31

His sovereignty on our behalf, because this is the love of God poured forth through the Holy Spirit in our hearts, we have for our future only the bold word *sōthēsometha* "we shall be saved" (vv. 9-10), and there is nothing left to us but to glory in our existence. On the death of God's Son there follows His life as the Risen One (v. 10). When we put our faith in God's righteous decision carried out in Him, we immediately become sharers in Christ's triumph —"how much more" (*pollō mallon*).

In this context Paul uses this phrase twice: "Since Christ died for us when we were yet sinners, *how much more* shall we"—on the ground of our justification which is already objectively complete—"be saved by Him" (vv. 8-9); and "Since, when we were yet enemies, we were reconciled to God through the death of His Son, *how much more* shall we, as the reconciled, be saved in His risen life" (v. 10). Here it is explicitly made clear that this argument from reconciliation to salvation is logically based upon the fact that Christ has not only died but has also risen. Ahead of us lies salvation, and—since, having shared His death, we must now share His life with Him as well—we can do nothing but glory in it. In particular, the stupendous fact that the believer may and must glory in his existence has its ground and meaning here. We glory "in God" (v. 11) when we glory in our hope (v. 2). Put concretely, that means that we glory "through our Lord Jesus," through His mouth and His voice, we glory in the glory which, as the resurrected from the dead, He proclaims. His risen life sets the seal upon the righteous decision of God effected in His death, and because He lives, this peace, and our reconciliation, and the pouring forth of the love of God in our hearts, mark a point in our journey beyond which there is no turning back, going on from which we have only one future, and in which we can only glory. His resurrection is the supreme act of God's sovereignty; henceforth we are bound to live and think in its light.

It is clear that although Paul sees Christ as belonging together with God and His work, he also sees Him as distinguished from God, and speaks, too, of His human nature. It is clear that he puts the man Jesus in His dying and rising on the one side, and himself and all other men (here, in the first place, believers), with their past, present, and future, on the other side. It is clear that he speaks of Him as a human individual and describes Him as such with unmistakable emphasis. But the existence of this human individual does not therefore exhaust itself in its individuality. The very existence of this individual is identical with a divine righteous decision which potentially includes an indefinite multitude of other men, so as to be manifest and effective in those who believe in Him in a way that is absolutely decisive for their past, present, and future. He reconciles them with God through His death. That means that in His own death He makes their peace with God—before they themselves have decided for this peace and quite apart from that decision. In believing, they are only conforming to the decision about them that has already been made in Him. What matters most to them is that they are no longer the enemies of God that they once were; ahead of them is future salvation instead of certain condemnation in the judgment of God's wrath; they have, also, the certain hope of sharing in God's own glory and can only glory in existing in such a hope. All that is due, not to their resolving and disposing, which rather tended in precisely the opposite direction, but to the fact that it was settled without and in spite of them, when He died on Golgotha and was raised up from the grave in the garden of Joseph of Arimathea. In believing in Him they are acknowledging that when He died and rose again, they too, died and rose again in Him, and that, from now on, their life, in its essentials, can only be a copy and image of His. It is He who *is* God's love toward them, and when this love of God is poured forth in their hearts through the Holy Spirit, that can only mean that He is in them and they in Him—and that happens quite independently of any prior love toward God from their side. Afterward, and because this has happened, they are of course asked about that also. But this must be understood quite literally: they glory even now "through Him," and only through Him (v. 11), in echo of the new glory of human existence proclaimed through His mouth. Apart from that, and of themselves, there would be nothing in human existence in which they could glory.

Such then is the status of this human individual. He is an individual in such a way that others are not only beside Him and along with Him, but in their most critical decision about their relationship to God, they are also and first of all *in* Him. His individuality is such therefore that with His being and doing, with His living and dying, a decision is made about them also, which at first is simply contrary to their own decision, and which afterward they can only acknowledge and carry out in their own decision. He pleads their cause, not merely as if it were His own, but, in and with His own cause, He in fact pleads theirs. He does that in such measure that it might well be asked how He Himself in His individuality could remain distinct from them. But it appears that His individual distinctness from them is preserved by the unique way in which He identifies Himself with them. And, at the same time, the precedence in origin and status between Him and them remains intact and irreversible. His function remains that of giving, theirs of receiving; His of leading the way, theirs of following. His position remains unchangeably that of original, theirs of copy. He remains unmistakably distinguished from any of them.

It is, however, first in vv. 12-21 that these relationships become quite clear. In this second half of the chapter, Paul goes farther than in the first half by setting the same material in a wider context. Here the new point is that the *special* anthropology of Jesus Christ—the one man for all men, all men in the one man—constitutes the secret of "Adam" also, and so is the *norm* of *all* anthropology. Paul now makes a fresh start with the question of the past out of which believers have come and in which they still have a part, and at the same time he takes up again the question of the totality of men whom, in vv.

6-10 he had first set over against Christ as weak, sinners, godless, enemies.

V. 12 has usually been taken as an anacoluthon.[2] More probably it should be taken as a kind of heading to what follows. *For this reason (dia touto)* are we such as vv. 1-11 described us, *for this reason* shall we be saved by sharing in the risen life of Jesus Christ, *for this reason* do we glory in our hope through Him—namely, that already as weak, sinners, godless, and enemies, already as children and heirs of Adam, and so in the past from which we came, we were not completely beyond the reach of the truth of Jesus Christ, but stood in a definite (even if negative) relationship to His saving power. V. 12 sets out this negative relationship. "As through one man sin has broken into the world, and through sin death, and as death has spread to all men, for that all men have sinned"—in other words, the relationship between Adam and all of us *then*, in the past, corresponds to the relationship between Christ and all of us *now*, in the present. Because of that correspondence it is true, as Paul has already emphasized

---

[2] "A sentence or expression in which the latter part does not syntactically carry out the construction begun in the first part" (Webster), a mannerism characteristic of Paul's way of speaking, probably because he dictated his letters.—Ed.

in vv. 6, 8, 10, that Christ died for us while we were still living in the unredeemed past with Adam. Because of it, even in that past we were not completely forsaken and lost. Because of it, we can now look back at that past with good cheer—and can therefore "so much the more" glory in our present, and in the future that opens out from it. We were not, even then, in an entirely different world. Even then, we existed in an order whose significance was of course just the opposite of that of the Kingdom of Christ, but which had the same structure.

When we look back we must and we may recognize the ordering principle of the Kingdom of Christ even in the ordering principle of the world of Adam. Even when we were weak, sinners, godless, enemies, though we were traveling in a very different direction, the rule of the road strikingly resembled—was indeed the same as—the one we know now. Between our former existence outside Christ and our present existence in Him there is a natural connection. Our former existence outside Christ is, rightly understood, already a still hidden but real existence in Him. Because of that, we dare to confess that we have peace with God, we dare to glory in our future salvation—we who still have that past, we who today are still the same men who were once weak, sinners, godless, and enemies. Our past cannot frighten us: in spite of it, and even taking it fully into account, we are still allowed and required to confess our reconciliation and glory in our salvation, just because our past as such—namely, the relationship between Adam and all of us—was already ordered so as to correspond to our present and future —namely, the relationship between Christ and all of us. That is what is made clear in the heading in v. 12.

The meaning of the famous parallel (so called) between "Adam and Christ," which now follows, is not that the relationship between Adam and us is the expression of our true and original nature, so that we would have to recognize in Adam the fundamental truth of anthropology to which the subsequent relationship between Christ and us would have to fit and adapt itself. The relationship between Adam and us reveals not the primary but only the secondary anthropological truth and ordering principle. The primary anthropological truth and ordering principle, which only mirrors itself in that relationship, is made clear only through the relationship between Christ and us. Adam is, as is said in v. 14, *typos tou mellontos*, the type of Him who was to come. Man's essential and original nature is to be found, therefore, not in Adam but in Christ. In Adam we can only find it prefigured. Adam can therefore be interpreted only in the light of Christ and not the other way round.

This then is our past—Adam and all of us, Adam in his relationship to us, we in our relationship to Adam. This is the history of man and of humanity outside Christ: the sin and death of a single man, of Adam, the man who in his own person is and represents the whole of humanity, the man in whose decision and destiny the decisions and destinies, the sins and the death of all the other men who come after him, are anticipated. It is also true that each of these others has lived his own life, has sinned his own sins, and has had to die his own death. Even so, the lives of all other men after Adam have only been the repetition and variation of his life, of his beginning and his end, of his sin and his death. That is our past. So were we weak, sinners, godless, and enemies, always Adam in us and ourselves in Adam, the one and the many, in the irremovable distinctness of the one over and against the others, in the irremovable unity of the others with the one. But now our past existence without Christ has no independent status or importance. Because it was constituted by this double relationship between the one and the others, it is now only the type, the likeness, the preliminary shadow of our present existence, which is itself constituted by the relationship between the One Christ and the many others and by the grace of God and His promise of life to men. Now the way in which our past was related to Adam can be understood only as a reflection and witness of the way in which our present is related to Christ. Human existence, as constituted by our relationship with Adam in our unhappy past as weak, sinners, godless, enemies, has no independent reality, status, or importance of its own. It is only an indirect witness to the reality of Jesus Christ and to the original and essential human existence that He inaugurates and reveals. The righteous decision of God has fallen upon men not in Adam but in Christ. But in Christ it has also fallen upon Adam, upon our relationship to him and so upon our unhappy past. When we know Christ, we also know Adam as the one who belongs to Him. The relationship that existed between Adam and us is, according to v. 12, the relationship that exists originally and essentially between Christ and us.

Paul's next point can best be understood by first passing on from v. 12 straight to vv. 18-19, and then to v. 21. These verses contain the parallel itself. V. 18: "As one man's trespass led to condemnation for all men, so one man's righteous act (*dikaiōma*) leads to the righteous decision which brings pardon and the promise of life (*dikaiōsis zōēs*, lit.: justification which leads to life) for all men." V. 19: "As by the one man's disobedience many were accounted sinners before God, so by one man's obedience many shall be accounted righteous." And then v. 21, which is a summary of the whole: "As sin reigned (i.e., held sway over all men) in death, so through the righteous decision grace reigns unto eternal life through Jesus Christ, our Lord." The parallel must first be seen as such. In both cases there is the one, and in both, the many, *all* men. Here, in Adam, is the one, who by what he is and does and undergoes, inaugurates, represents, and reveals what the many, *all* men who come after him, will also have to be and do and undergo. But here, in Adam, are also the many, *all* men, not one of them the less guilty or the less penalized because he is not himself the one, but each rather finding himself completely in what the one is and does and undergoes, and recognizing himself only too clearly in him. There, in Christ, is, for the first time in the true sense, the One who stands, as such, for all the others. He also is the

Inaugurator, Representative, and Revealer of what through Him and with Him the many, *all* men shall also be, do, and receive. And there, also for the first time in the true sense, are the many, *all* men, not one of them less righteous or less blessed because he is not himself the One, but each rather finding and recognizing himself again in what this One who takes his place is, and does, and has received. As in the existence of the one, here in Adam, the result for the many, *all* men, is the lordship of sin, and, with it, the destiny of death; so again, in the exist- ence of the One, there in Christ, the result for all men is the lordship of grace exercised in the divine righteous decision and the promise of eternal life.

That is a general summary of the relationships laid down in vv. 18-19, 21. The parallel is formally complete. In 1 Cor. 15:21-22 also, Paul first makes this formal parallel clear: "As death came through one man, so also the resurrection came through one man. For as in Adam all die, so in Christ shall all be made alive." That is the situation of man here with Adam and man there with Christ. Thus both sides—"Adam and all of us" and "Christ and all of us"—are from the start closely connected, and we immediately become aware of that connection when we see that the same formal relationship that once bound us to Adam now binds us to Christ.

This formal parallel is, however, not Paul's only concern. Taken by itself, it leaves the material relationship between Christ and Adam still undefined. We still do not know whether, on one side or the other, there is an essential priority and an inner superiority that would make Christ the master of Adam or Adam the master of Christ. Perhaps sin and death are as strong as grace and life. Perhaps they will ultimately prove stronger. It remains still an open question whether Adam or Christ tells us more about the true nature of man. Perhaps it is Adam who embodies basic human nature as it appears in all its many possible forms whereas Christ only embodies it in the one form in which it appears in Christian or religious men: perhaps Christ only tells us the truth about Christians, whereas Adam tells us the truth about all men. But when we look again at Rom. 5, we find that Paul does not deal with the formal parallel between the two sides in isolation, but in a context where their material relationship is made unambiguously clear. Even in vv. 18-19, 21, Paul does not leave it an open question whether Adam is prior to Christ or Christ is superior to Adam. He does not leave the two side by side in a merely formal relationship. It is not enough for him to show that life in Christ helps to explain life in Adam. He is also concerned to make quite clear the material relationship of these two formally parallel sides, so that no uncertainty can remain.

We have already seen that on both sides there is the formal identity of the one human nature which is not annulled or transformed even by sin. But in reaching that conclusion we are bound to recognize that the formal identity itself depends upon the greatest possible material disparity between the two sides. For what we have said about Adam and the rest of us is only valid because it corresponds with what we already know about Christ and the rest of us so that it is Christ who vouches for the authenticity of Adam and not Adam who vouches for the authenticity of Christ.

Therefore the status of Adam is lower than the status of Christ, the sin of Adam counts for less than the righteousness of Christ. So also the relationship of the many to Adam is less significant than their other relationship to Christ. The only thing that is *common* to both relationships is that in two different contexts true human nature is revealed, and that in two different ways it is shown to be subject to the ordering of God its Creator. But to discover this common factor that connects the two sides, we have to take into account the decisive difference between them. And this difference is that our relationship to Adam is only the type, the likeness, the preliminary shadow of our relationship to Christ. The same human nature appears in both but the humanity of Adam is only real and genuine in so far as it reflects and corresponds to the humanity of Christ.

"The first man is of the earth, earthy, the second man is from heaven." That is how Paul puts it in 1 Cor. 15:47. Christ is above, Adam is beneath. Adam is true man only because he is below and not above, because his claim to be the "first man" and the head of humanity like Christ is only apparent. We are truly men because we, like Adam, are below and not above, because Adam's claim to be our head and to make us members in his body is only apparent. We are real men in our relationship to Adam, only because Adam is not our head and we are not his members, because above Adam and before Adam is Christ. Our relationship to Christ has an essential priority and superiority over our relationship to Adam. He is the Victor and we in Him are those who are awaiting the victory. Our human nature is preserved by sharing Adam's nature, because Adam's humanity is a *provisional copy* of the real humanity that is in Christ. And so as Adam's children and heirs, in our past as weak, sinners, godless, and enemies, we are in this provisional way still men whose nature reflects the true human nature of Christ. And so, because our nature in Adam is a provisional copy of our true nature in Christ, its formal structure can and must even in its perversion be the same.

The whole argument turns on this provisional character of Adam and of our human nature in its relation to him. Right from the start we have to take account of the essential disparity between him and Christ, and between our bond with him and our bond with Christ. This is not a case of right against right, but of man's wrong against God's right, not of truth against truth, but of man's lie against God's truth. It is not even a case of power against power, but of man's powerlessness against God's power. Least of all is it a case of God against God—a god of this world against God the Creator—but simply of man against the one God, and, on the other side, the same one God for man. That is why we cannot rest content with the formal parallel and why the question about the priority and superiority of one side over the other can only be answered in one way. The main point of Rom. 5:12-21 is that here man stands against God in such a way that, even in his opposition, his wrongness, his lie, and his powerlessness, he must be a witness for God, that even as Adam and Adam's child he must be the mirror that reflects God's work, and so be the precursor of Christ. Even in his *bad* relationship to Adam, he still remains man, and the structure of his nature is such that it can find its meaning and fulfillment in his *good* relationship to Christ. Even under the lordship of *sin* and *death* his nature is still human nature and so is the image and likeness of what it will be under the lordship of *grace* and *life*. That is how the essential disparity between Adam and Christ is contained within their formal identity. Our relationship to Adam is a subordinate relationship, because the guilt and punishment we incur in Adam have no independent reality of their own but are only the dark shadows of the grace and life we find in Christ.

That is the point which Paul is making clear in the middle section, vv. 15-17. The point here is that when we compare man's relationship to Adam with his relationship to Christ, although the two are formally symmetrical, there is really the greatest and most fundamental disparity between them. It should be noticed that this passage comes before vv. 18-19, in which the parallel is developed. Paul himself has not adopted our procedure of getting a clear outline of the whole by first concentrating upon the formal identity of the two sides and then going on to explain their essential disparity. What he sees and says first is rather that our relationship to Adam is completely different from and subordinate to our relationship to Christ. It is by first emphasizing the disparity that he comes to recognize the identity as well. The parallel between the one and the many, the *heis* and the *polloi*, on both sides in vv. 18-19 is introduced as a corollary of the disparity between them, as the inferential "then" (*ara oun*) of v. 18 shows. Paul sums up that disparity in two statements which have the same construction, and which taken together make his meaning clear.

The first of these is in v. 15*a: oukh hōs to paraptōma, houtōs to charisma*—literally: "It is not the same with grace as it is with the transgression." In other words, grace is not to be measured by sin; in spite of the formal identity between them, the sin of Adam is not comparable with the grace of Christ. V. 15*b* gives the reason for this statement. It is, of course, true that the sin (*paraptōma = peccatum*) of the one Adam, brought about the death of the many, not only as its consequence but as something directly involved in itself. It is true that there and then, with sin, death also broke into the world of men (v. 12), so that there and then the many died, even before they were born. But over and against that stands the other truth that in the grace of the other One, the man Jesus, the grace of God overflowed upon these many who were already dead in and with the sin of Adam. Why "overflowed"? Because Adam's sin is only Adam's sin, but the grace of Jesus Christ is the grace of *God* and His gift. And so *eperisseusen*, it overflowed, it prevailed, it was greater than sin. Thus, when the work of Christ is compared with the work of Adam, though they are formally identical, yet the difference between them is the radical, final, and irremovable difference between God and man. That is why v. 15a said that the grace (*charisma*) was not to be measured by the transgression (*paraptōma*). That is why the opposite alone is possible. Paul is not denying that Adam's sin still brings death to all men, but he is affirming that the grace of Christ has an incomparably greater power to make these dead men alive. He is not saying that there is no truth in Adam, but he is saying that it is a subordinate truth that depends for its validity on its correspondence with the final truth that is in Christ.

The second of our two statements is in v. 16a: *kai*

oukh hōs di'henos hamartēsantos to dōrēma—literally: "It is not the same with the gift [given us through the grace of God] as it is with what has come upon us through the one who sinned." In other words, the result of grace is not to be measured by the result of sin; in spite of the formal identity between them, the effect of Adam's sin is not comparable with the effect of Christ's grace. The supporting argument in vv. 16*b*-17 is more detailed than in v. 15. It is arranged in two contrasts between Christ and Adam, the first of which prepares the way for the second. V. 16*b* contains this introductory contrast. What has come upon us through the one who first sinned (*ex henos*) is judgment (*krima*) which inevitably led to punishment (*katakrima*). In and with him we are found guilty and condemned. That is the result of sin. What that means in practice will be explained more closely in v. 17. In v. 16*b* it is first contrasted with the completely different result of grace. Grace (*charisma*) enters in just at the point where the work of sin, which started in the one, has been completed in the many, so that in their relationship to the one all men have now sinned and become guilty and ripe for condemnation (v. 12). The place where grace makes its first contact with men is in the transgressions of many, the *paraptōmata pollōn*, and that is the very place where sin justifies its claim that all men are guilty in and with Adam, and renders them liable to Adam's condemnation. It is not strange that sin should bring judgment and judgment condemnation in its train. But it is very strange that at the precise point where sin has brought all men under condemnation, grace should intervene, so that what actually follows the *paraptōmata pollōn* (the transgressions of many) is not the condemnation of sin, but its very opposite, the pardon of God. *Paraptōmata—dikaiōma*, sin—pardon, the pardon after which the *katakrima* that follows the *krima* is not taken into account any more. "There is now therefore no condemnation (*katakrima*) for those who are in Christ Jesus" (Rom. 8:1). But how can sin lead to pardon, how can we pass *ek pollōn paraptōmatōn eis dikaiōma* (from many transgressions into justification)? Is it not impossible to find a way to pardon from sin? V. 16*b* leads us to the question by showing us that although it is easy to understand how sin leads to condemnation, it is impossible to understand how grace can lead to pardon for sinful men. But it is v. 17 that gives the real reason for the statement in v. 16*a*. It should be noted that v. 17 has the same grammatical construction as v. 15*b*: *ei gar tō tou henos paraptōmati....* (if through one man's transgressions. . . .). The thing, on the one side, that we can understand, and the thing, on the other, that we cannot understand, are now named. The external disparity of the two sides, which is indicated in v. 16*b*, is now explained by bringing out what actually happens when sin and grace set to work among men.

What is this *katakrima*, this punishment or condemnation? Paul's answer is that it is the lordship of death. By the transgression of the one that lordship has been established and is now being exercised. And through that one it is lordship over the many as well, and all the more so because the many also have sinned, each for himself. To say that death rules over all men is not the same as to say, with v. 15*b*, that all men have died. It emphasizes that death is an objective and alien power that is now exercising its lordship over man. Death, like sin, is an intruder into human life; in the original scheme for man's world it had no place at all. When sin broke into the world (v. 12), death found the way by which it could claim all men. That is what happens when as a result of his sin man is condemned. Death is not so much God's direct reaction against man's sin; it is rather God's abandoning of the men who have abandoned Him. Think of the Book of

Judges; as soon as Israel turns to strange gods, it is immediately abandoned to the hostile power of alien peoples. With God's rule there goes also God's protection, and when Israel cast off that protection, its danger and helplessness are immediately made clear. That is what it means in practice for man's sin to be condemned. Through the one who sinned there has come upon us the unnatural oppression and constraint of death, which becomes inevitable where man has cast off his obedience to God. As we saw in v. 16*b*, the logical connection between sin and condemnation is easy to understand, but the practical outcome of death ruling over human life is so unnatural that it is impossible to understand it at all. Its complete contrast to that is the practical significance of the *dikaiōma* (righteous decision, justifying act). Here grace overflows on all men (v. 15*b*) and they receive the *dōrea tēs dikaiosunēs*, God's free gift of righteousness, and the result is that instead of death ruling over them, they themselves are going *to rule in life* with God—*en zōē basileusousin*.

Men who are already under the alien lordship of death and are already dead in their sins, are rescued from that situation and transferred into a completely different situation, in which instead of dying an alien death, they will live their own true life and so will not be slaves but lords. This is the situation which has already been described as our future salvation in vv. 9-10, and as our hope of sharing in God's glory in v. 2. We have already seen that where the *dikaiōmo* (righteous act) intervenes on the *krima* (judgment), there is no more *katakrima* (condemnation). But now we can go farther than this: the *dikaiōma* is the *dikaiōma* of God. And so there goes with it hope, the greatest hope of all, the hope of the glory of God, the hope of the *basileuein en zōē* (ruling in life)—of living the true kingly life of man. This hope, though it is indeed marvelous that men condemned to death should ever come to enjoy it, is the natural result of God's pardon, and to live in this hope is the natural condition of man, that is, of the man who is righteous in the eyes of God. What could be more obvious than that a righteous man should be able to live in this hope of sharing the glory of God?

This, then, is the difference between the result of sin and the result of grace, namely, the free gift, the *dōrēma*. As we saw in v. 16*b*, the logical connection between sin and pardon is impossible to understand, but the practical result that man receives life and lives it is so natural that it can be understood without any difficulty at all. We can now see the disparity between the result of grace and the result of sin, and so once more, in a new way, the disparity between man in Adam and man in Christ. It should be clearly noted that here also there is no question of denying or annulling the truth in Adam. Paul both looks back to the place where death *ruled, ebasileusen,* as well as looking forward to the place where men *will rule, basileusousin,* in life (v. 17). He has accurately recognized and explained both results in their inner nature and at the same time has given each its due place. For the two results are quite different. On the one side the logical connection between sin and death is unmistakably obvious, but the practical outcome of the rule of death is impossibly strange: while on the other side the logical connection between sin and pardon is completely miraculous and the material outcome of men living their true life is natural and true to the fundamental nature of man. These glaring contrasts make the difference between the two results quite plain. The result of sin is to destroy human nature, the result of grace is to restore it, so that it is obvious that sin is subordinate to grace, and that it is grace that has the last word about the true nature of man.

We may sum up Paul's two arguments for the disparity between Christ and Adam as follows: The

first is in v. 15, the second in vv. 16-17; the nerve
of the first and shorter argument is that on the one
side it is man who acts, and on the other God in all
His finality; the nerve of the second and more detailed argument is that although our relationship
with Christ is formally the same as our relationship
with Adam, yet in external context, internal content,
in logical structure and in practical outcome, the two
are completely different and diametrically opposed.

But we have not yet noticed an important element
in this central section of the passage. At first sight it
appears to be of no importance, but to consider it
will bring to light yet another essential factor in this
situation. This is the *pollō mallon*, the "how much
more," which first appears in vv. 9-10 and is taken
up again in the important vv. 15-17. This formula
is the key to the relationship of the two sides and to
the meaning of the contrast between them. The remarkable thing about it is that it both connects its
two terms and subordinates the one to the other. So
in this case it both presupposes and affirms the identity of the two sides, and at the same time uses this
presupposition to make their disparity clear.

Whenever it is possible to use the phrase "much
more" in comparing one thing with another, we are
dealing with two things that fall under the same

ordering principle, which is valid and recognizable in lesser degree on the one side, and in greater degree on the other. If it was not first valid on one side, it could not be "so much more" valid on the other. If it was not first clearly recognized on one side, it could not be "so much more" clearly recognized on the other. In our context, the first term in the comparison is the entire realm of the truth in Adam, in which, according to vv. 15-17, the many die in the transgression of the one, because through the transgression of the one death has gained lordship over all men. About this truth in Adam the *pollō mallon* makes one thing clear. It tells us that it stands under the same ordering principle as the truth in Christ, and that even though the truth in Adam is subordinate to the truth in Christ, yet in it that principle is valid and can be recognized.

To understand why this can and must be so, we have to refer back to the use of the same formula in vv. 9-10. There the first term of the comparison, which is put, so to speak, on the left-hand side, is our reconciliation through the death of Christ when we were still weak, sinners, godless, and enemies. Since, we are told in vv. 9-10, this first term on the left-hand side is valid, "how much more" valid is the second term on the right-hand side, which is our hope of salvation through the resurrection of Christ from the dead. And so both reconciliation and salvation are grounded on the same ordering principle, and both find a common validity in the one work of Christ, in the humiliation and exaltation of this one man. And within that work of Christ both can be recognized, the distinction between them stands, for it is because we are sure that Christ achieved our reconciliation that we can be "so much more" sure that He has achieved our salvation as well. In vv. 15-17 the first term on the left-hand side, the sin of Adam and its result, seems to have nothing in common with the second term on the right, the grace of Jesus Christ and the gift it brings. In fact the one seems as different from the other as darkness is from light. But here, as before, the *pollō mallon* forms a bond and a link and points to an ordering principle that can connect even such opposites as these. And it is because *pollō mallon* first connects the two terms in vv. 9-10, that it can also connect the opposites of vv. 15-17.

The death and the resurrection of Jesus Christ, our reconciliation through His blood on the one hand, and our hope in the power of His life on the other, are two aspects—two very different aspects, it is true—of one single action. For that reason, in

vv. 15-17 also, it is not enough merely to distinguish the truth in Adam from the truth in Christ. Because there is a valid and recognizable connection between Christ's death for sinners and His rising to bring life to men, there must also be a valid and recognizable connection between Adam in whom men sin and die and Christ in whom they are pardoned and made alive. The only connection between Christ and Adam is that for Adam Christ died and rose again. From the sin of Adam, as such, no way leads to the grace of Christ, no way from *krima* (judgment) to *dikaiōma* (righteousness), no way from *katakrima* (condemnation) to *sōtēria* (salvation), no way from death to life. If we looked from left to right, we would find every attempt to move in that direction frustrated, every door closed. If we could regard Adam and our participation in his sin and condemnation as an isolated and self-centered whole, then it would be impossible to find there any connection with Christ and our participation in His grace and life.

But so to regard Adam is impossible. Paul does not go to Adam to see how he is connected with Christ; he goes to Christ to see how *He* is connected with Adam. Already in vv. 9-10 he has looked *back* at our unhappy past, and in so doing has brought it into positive relation with our present and future, which at first sight seemed to have nothing in common with it at all. The present and future belong to Christ and in belonging to Christ they are connected with the past, because the past contains not only Adam's sin and Adam's death, not only our weakness, sin, godlessness, and enmity, it contains also the crucifixion of Jesus Christ, and through it our reconciliation to God. It is because Christ has thus invaded the world of Adam and claimed it for Himself, that Paul can find a connection between the two, a way that leads from Adam to Christ for himself and all believers, *prosagōgē eis tēn charin tautēn, en hē hestēkamen* (an access to this grace in which we in fact stand [v. 2]). Thus in vv. 15-17 Paul cannot treat the truth in Adam as though it were independent and self-contained. The truth in Christ will not allow it to be that, for Christ has challenged the right of sin and death to rule over Adam's world, by invading that world and making it His own. Only by overlooking or forgetting the truth in Christ which has broken into the world of Adam, could we judge the truth in Adam to be absolutely without light. It has, of course, no light of its own. But it is drawn into the light by the fact that Jesus Christ is risen from the dead. And when that light shines, it shows us the cross on which the same Jesus Christ suffered and died for the sin of Adam and the sin of all men, and by which Adam and all men are reconciled and pardoned and can find again the now reopened way to life with God.

The same Jesus Christ is already involved in the truth in Adam, which in our treatment of *pollō mallon* we put on the left-hand side of the comparison. He is already in the midst of the world of sin and death, which for our power and our knowledge is a closed circle beyond whose bounds we cannot pass. In that world He is already King, secretly in His humiliation. Already He disputes Adam's miserable right to represent and make valid against Him a distinct truth of his own. He disputes also the right of all others, who have sinned with Adam. He steps into Adam's place and into our place with the claim, the right, and the power, to make our sin and our death His responsibility, and so to pronounce God's pardon and remove the *katakrima* from the world, bringing in instead of it the promise in power. Because the truth in Christ has this superiority in power over the truth in Adam, the two stand together under one ordering principle. That is why it is legitimate to relativize the opposition between them in such a remarkable way by the *pollō mallon* of vv. 15-17.

Christ and Adam

And that is why it is relevant to go on in vv. 15-19 to point out the formal parallel between the *heis* (one) and the *polloi* (many) on both sides. That parallel is no mere playing with words and ideas, because the one Jesus Christ who took Adam's place in His death on the cross, has thereby entered into the closest possible relationship with Adam, and, since, in dying for the one Adam, He died also for the many who had sinned in Adam. He has thereby entered into the closest possible relationship with them.

The parallel between Adam and Christ in the construction of vv. 18-19 is justified and made necessary by the fact that although Adam has no power to identify himself with Christ, Christ has the power (vv. 15-17) to identify Himself with Adam, and so to establish the formal identification upon which the parallel rests. The close relationship of the two sides is established, not by trying to find a way from Adam to Christ, but by seeing that Christ has found the only way to Adam by His cross. And since Christ has passed from His side into the world of Adam, Adam is now free to pass into the world of Christ; Christ has removed the barriers and opened the doors and Adam can pass from sin to pardon—from death to life. Of this direct connection opened up between the two sides, Paul makes legitimate use in vv. 18-19.

The significant phrase *pollō mallon* has now to be explained on its other side as well. The formula not only joins its terms together but also subordinates one to the other. Whenever it is possible to use the phrase "so much more" in comparing one thing with another, we are dealing with two things that fall under the same ordering principle, which is valid and recognizable in lesser degree on the one side and in greater degree on the other. Since it is already valid and recognizable even on the first side, it must be "all the more" valid and recognizable on the other side as well. For if it is already valid and recognizable on the one side, where its presence is a mystery, how could it not be ever "so much more" valid and recognizable on the other side, where this mystery does not arise? The second term of the comparison is in our case the truth in Christ described in vv. 15-17; it is the grace of God which in the one Jesus Christ overflows upon the many who had sinned and were dead in Adam; it is the incomprehensible yet unmistakable and irrevocable *dikaiōma* (justifying act) which first begins to operate in relation to the *paraptōmata tōn pollōn* (transgressions of the many); it is the expectation of a kingly life in the glory of

Christian and Adam

God—the life that has taken the place of the *kata-krima* (condemnation) which inevitably threatened man. The *pollō mallon* makes clear that we can "all the more" surely recognize the validity of this truth in Christ, because it is already recognizable even in the subordinate world of Adam, where it seems so questionable and open to doubt. If the truth in Christ holds good in the dark and alien world of Adam, "how much more" does it hold good in the world of Christ, where it really and originally belongs! If it can shine in the darkness where it seems impossible for it to shine, "how much more" can it shine in the brightness to which it belongs! We can be all the surer of it here with Christ, because we can already be sure of it there with Adam, even if only in an indirect and subsidiary way.

To understand this we have to go back once more to the use of the same formula in vv. 9-10. There, the second term of the comparison is *zōē* (life)—the resurrection of Christ, the future salvation it brings us, and our hope of sharing in the glory of God. It is the grace in which, according to v. 2, we have taken our stand. And, says vv. 9-10, this *zōē* is "all the more" certain, because the other term of the comparison—our reconciliation through Christ's death when we were weak, sinners, godless, and enemies—is already certain and sure. To that we might reply that it is by no means sure or certain that Christ's death has brought reconciliation to men; the world is still as ignorant as ever of what Christ did for men. Men are still sinners, who do not know that Christ died for them and that they are therefore reconciled sinners; sinners, who make no thankful response to God's grace, but still go on rejecting it: sinners who still cry "Crucify Him!" and commit all over again the very sins that Christ bore away, sinners who all over again make themselves liable to the death that He suffered for them, and from which they have already been rescued by His death on the cross. That is the real dark mystery that surrounds our reconciliation, which Christ claims to have accomplished once and for all. And the heart of the mystery is that we are thus left in our ignorance, because here amidst the sin of the world even Christ Himself seems to win no triumph, but is present in His complete humiliation. This is the place where sinful man, where Church and State, where we in our ingratitude, successfully stand out against Him. There is nothing there to stop us. Nothing happens to open our eyes, to rescue us from our ignorance. Sin takes its course. The *krima* (judgment) is pronounced and not revoked, the *katakrima* (condemnation) follows with a relentless logic that is only too easy to understand. Christ suffers, dies, and is buried. . . .

But we have forgotten the very thing that we ought not to forget—namely, that it was at the very moment when this happened that we were reconciled, and that our reconciliation is no less real or valid because that was how it came about. On the contrary, unless we had been reconciled amidst the darkness of the mystery of sin, we could not have been reconciled at all. Is Christ less Christ because He is present only in His humiliation? How else can He be completely Christ except in His complete humiliation? And is He not completely Christ here, because here in His utter loneliness He is abandoned by all? How else could He be the Christ who is for all? Could He be exalted, were He not also thus humiliated? Must not He always be acknowledged, even in His exaltation, as the Christ who was humiliated by all, and also by us, and so as the Christ who was humiliated for all and also for us? Is it surprising that here our relation to Him is terrible ignorance? Would we be the sinners for whom He had to die and did die, if it were otherwise? No, this is the only way in which our reconciliation can be valid and real. This is the only way in which there can break in upon the dark world of sin the light of Easter Day. In that darkness our reconciliation has taken place, God's righteous decision has been carried out, Adam's pardon and ours has been pronounced in spite of his sin and the *paraptōmata tōn pollōn* (transgressions of the many). God's decision for us has here been made completely and entirely in opposition to us. "All we like sheep have gone astray; we have turned every one to his own way, but the Lord hath laid on Him the iniquity of us all" (Is. 53:6). The place where He bore our iniquity must be a dark place. But into that darkness there shines the bright light of Easter, because there He bore our iniquity for our salvation and to the glory of God. And if, when it is seen in that light, even our unhappy past is made bright, "how much more" bright is our present over which the light of Easter shines without any darkness at all. For its brightness shines also on our past, so that indirectly and subsequently we have to acknowledge that here in the darkness (where all was done without us and in spite of us and so, in reality, for us) Christ's decisive work, which has absolute superiority over Adam's work and all its results for ever, has been performed. That happened in the humiliation of Christ, in which He is to all eternity our Saviour and

King. It happened in His blood in the power of which He intercedes for us as the Risen and Exalted Lord. And so, if the light of Easter, falling indirectly on our past, makes it clear that in that past our salvation and hope have their eternally unshakable foundation, "how much more" sure and certain are that salvation and hope when we see them in the same light's direct and unreflected blaze!

From that we can go on to understand the significance of *pollō mallon* in vv. 15-17. In these verses also, the second term is "all the more" certain, because the first term on the left is already certain and sure. This first term here is Adam's sin, of which we have become guilty by our sinning in Adam, and Adam's death, which by our sinning we also deserve to die. Again at a first glance we have good reason to be surprised. Would not "how much less" be more in place than Paul's astonishing "how much more"? How can we be sure of God's grace in this situation? On the contrary, could anything make us surer of the disgrace of man? Where is there here a *prosagōgē eis tēn charin* (access to grace)? Here the weak, the sinners, the godless, the enemies, are clearly on their own ground, and the only thing we can be sure of is the wrath of God. Here the only thing that seems appropriate is the monotonous alternation of accusations and threats that is found in so many prophetic passages of the Old Testament. "Adam and us," taken by itself, is an endless chapter which makes completely comfortless reading. But, as we have seen, this chapter is not to be read by itself, just as the Old Testament is not to be read by itself. Here, too, we must not forget the context in which the whole truth in Adam stands. By itself it is falsehood, and only in the fact that it is related to the truth in Christ has it any validity at all. But when we see Adam's world in the context of Christ's world, we discover how its isolation and the apparently endless accusations and threats against it can at last be brought to an end. Who, according to v. 16, is the man on whom God's grace has overflowed in Christ? The man who is already dead in Adam's sinful fall. It is to these dead men that God's grace is shown. Who are those who, according to v. 16, are justified through God's power? The many who by their transgressions have shown that the guilt and condemnation of Adam is by right their own. It is these condemned men that God has justified. Who are those who, according to v. 17, are *basileusontes tē zōē* (those who will reign in life)? The very men over whom death became the uncontested king. It is the slaves of death that are to become the lords of life.

Behind the antithesis of vv. 9-10 there lies no frivolous dialectic. On the contrary, these are things that can and must be said. As we saw in vv. 9-11, those sinful and dying men, those condemned and enslaved men, are not alone, but Jesus Christ is in the midst of them, the Friend of publicans and sinners, who was crucified between the two thieves, who in free obedience was willing to identify Himself with Adam and his children and heirs and has identified Himself with them once and for all. And since He is in their midst, it is their self-will and their self-sufficiency that are the mystery; the sin of Adam, that makes His presence with Adam a mystery, itself becomes mysterious. Men who share the sin of Adam have become men who share the grace of Christ, men who belong to Adam now belong to Christ. It is once more from the Risen and Exalted Christ that the light breaks through the darkness to shine on Adam and his children and heirs. He who rose is also He who was crucified, and He who identified Himself with those who shared in Adam's sin. That is why His light is so penetrating. That is why it reveals sinners and dying men as those on whose behalf Christ intervened on the cross. That is why it reveals righteous and living men where by ourselves we can see nothing but these sinful and dying men. The truth in Adam can stand only because it points beyond its own comfortless message about human sin and death to the truth in Christ, which towers over it in its superiority. The truth in Adam is valid, not because of any intrinsic quality of its own, but only in its relationship to the truth in Christ which is above it; the truth in Christ establishes its own validity in its relation to what lies below it, by making the truth in Adam transparent, and turning it into a reflection of itself. But now it is no longer from that reflection that we recognize the truth. Now we know it not only in the context of Adam's fall where it is surrounded by so much mystery. The truth is transparent and reflected in this mysterious context because in faith we know the Risen and Exalted Lord.

Because we know Christ the Conqueror, we can also know Christ the Crucified. Because we know Adam and ourselves as men who are pardoned and who are going to share God's glory, we can also know Adam and ourselves as sinners who were once condemned to die. Now we live in the full light of the truth of Christ. Because of that the one who is our Head is not the captive, but the Liberator. Because of that we, the many, are not Adam's fellow captives, but those whom Christ has set free. Now it is not for us either to be dismayed by the hopelessness of the truth in Adam (when viewed in isolation) or to try perversely to make it look better than it is. Now it has already been brightened—just as it is in all its entire hopelessness. Now we look into the light which has made it bright. Now we know that there is reality and truth in Adam, and so there must all the more be reality and truth in Christ. Now is Christ risen—and by His resurrection He has revealed to us the victory and the reconciliation He has already achieved in the hiddenness of His death on the cross. Now we know that He has reconciled us, because even when we were dead in sin, He died to save us from judgment and condemnation and to make an end of the power of death. Now, after that past, the present, the time of the Messiah, has dawned, and has delivered the past from its emptiness and lostness by revealing it as the time in which Christ died to make the present a time of grace and pardon for men. And if the truth in Christ can prove its validity even when it is hidden amidst the sin and death of the world of Adam, "how much more" does it hold good in the world of grace and life where it properly and originally belongs! If in the light of Easter we can see Christ amidst the darkness of Adam's world, "how much more" clearly can we see Him in His own world where that light has its source! If the truth in Christ is valid and recognizable in the reflection it casts into the past, "how much more" valid and recognizable it is when it is seen, not in an indirect reflection, but clearly and directly in all its present reality and power!

We can now bring together what we have learnt from vv. 15-17 about the essential disparity between Christ and Adam. Our unity with Adam is less essential and less significant than our true unity with Christ. On both sides there are the same formal relationships between the one and the many, so that both sides have the same ordering principle. But within that formal identity, Adam is subordinate, because he can only be the forerunner, the witness, the preliminary shadow and likeness, the *typos* (type) [v. 14] of the Christ who is to come. Because he is that, because he is really like Christ, vv. 18-19 and 21 can go on to draw a valid and significant parallel between the two. The *pollō mallon* (much more) of vv. 15, 17, in its first meaning, has already made it clear that the two sides do belong together in that way. But within this belonging together there is a disparity. For Christ who seems to come second, really comes first, and Adam who seems to come first really comes second. In Christ the relationship between the one and the many is original, in Adam it is only a copy of that original. Our relationship to Adam depends for its reality on our relationship to Christ. And that means, in practice, that to find the true and essential nature of man we have to look not to Adam the fallen man, but to Christ in whom what is fallen has been cancelled and what was original has been restored. We have to correct and interpret what we know of Adam by what we know of Christ, because Adam is only true man in so far as he reflects and points to the original humanity of Christ.

In vv. 13-14 and in v. 20, Paul goes on to consider the disparity between Adam and Christ in its relation to the Law, and it is in this way that he makes the relationship between the two sides unambiguously clear. It is in this passage about the Law that Adam's significance as *typos tou mellontos* (a type of the coming one) is first recognized. Between Adam and Christ there stands Moses. Between the sin and death of man, on the one side, and the grace of God, on the other, there stands the revelation of God's will to His people Israel. What effect does the Law of Moses have on the relationship between Adam and Christ? Does the intervention of the Law between them destroy their relationship to each other and make all that has already been said about it radically false and wrong? It is these two questions that Paul is facing and answering in vv. 13-14 and 20.

When God reveals Himself through Moses to His people Israel—when Paul speaks of Moses he is thinking of the entire content of the Old Testament —He again confronts man in the same way as, according to Gen. 3, he once confronted Adam. The hidden, forgotten truth that all human history is essentially the history of God's covenant with man, is revealed and openly proclaimed in the history of Israel by the mouth of Moses and the prophets. Here God reveals Himself explicitly and over and over again in the midst of the daily life and experience of men. Here man lives once again—like Adam in Paradise—in a special, indeed in a unique way, in God's presence, and so in a holy place. Here man himself is sanctified by the manifestation of God's favor toward him and also by the restraint of God's command upon him.

The history of Israel is the story of God's dealings with Adam—and of Adam's dealings with God— expanded so that it covers the continuing life of a whole people; the story of Adam is the history of

Israel contracted into the life story of a single man. For both in the story of Adam and in the history of Israel, man's response to God's revelation is the same. In both he lets himself be enticed away by the voice of the stranger, he rebels against the God who has been revealed to him, he becomes disobedient and is made subject to the power of death. That is what happens when God chooses Israel out of all the other nations to reveal to it alone His will for men. That is what happens among the people in whom it is revealed that the history of humanity is the history of God's covenant with man. Here in Israel are revealed the *paraptōmata tōn pollōn* (transgressions of the many) and the inevitable *krima* (judgment) and *katakrima* (condemnation) that follow in their train.

The whole history of Israel in all its stages is the revelation of man's sin, *epi tō homoiōmati tēs parabaseōs Adam* (in the likeness of Adam's transgression [v. 14]) in shameful identification with the sin committed by Adam in Gen. 3. Nowhere else does it become so plain that the history of humanity, for all its changes and progress, is always and everywhere the history of the sin and condemnation of men. The place where God sets man apart for Himself in such a special way, where He is so specially present and gracious, where He makes it so specially

77

clear what He will have of him, is the very place where, in the light of God's Law, sin *ellogeitai* (v. 13) —literally, is substantiated as such, registered, laid to account. Here, where it is once and for all put on record that God is gracious, it has also to be recorded that man is a sinner. That is a conclusion from which the history of Israel allows no escape.

God's dealings with Israel make it impossible either to conceal or to explain away the fact that man is sinful, hard as it is for us to admit that that is true. The Old Testament is witness to God's revelation in that it presents this burdensome truth without concealment or extenuation, naked and bare. It is God's Word because it represents Israel as a people that is completely perverted and lost, because its verdict on man is the same as the verdict of the prophets in their endless accusations and threats. Not that other peoples have not also sinned in Adam, not that humanity outside Israel has not also shared Adam's fall. Paul does not say a single word to suggest that the Jews were or are worse than the others, or that the others were or are better than the Jews. On the contrary, he has explicitly reminded us: *achri gar nomou hamartia ēn en kosmō: sin was in the world before the Law came,* before there was any question of that special and visible recapitulation of the history of Adam in the election of Israel. In v. 12, Paul already has made it clear that "all have sinned," that is to say, that all have repeated Adam's sinful act. There is no excuse for any presumption on the part of Gentiles who lack the distinction of the Jews, no excuse for scorning the Jews who were honored by this distinction—although they were smitten by it as well. Death ruled already *apo Adam mechri Mōuseōs* (from Adam to Moses) over sinful men; it ruled over the Gentiles around Israel, just as much as in Israel itself (v. 14). The *paraptō-mata* were and are committed at all times and in all places, and so the *krima* and the *katakrima* apply not only to Israel but to all men. The special thing that happens only in Israel, the thing that distinguishes it from its predecessors and neighbors, is that here only there is a clear revelation of the graciousness of God and the sinfulness of man. Here only the *ellogein* (laying to account) takes place; the whole history of Israel is a unique working out of this *ellogein,* this substantiating and registering of human sin.

That is something that cannot be said about the history of the men and peoples before and around Israel. There also men have sinned, and so there also death rules. But there is no Law there, no revelation of God's will to show us this sinning as what it is, to make it known that death is God's condemnation upon men: *hamartia de oukh ellogeitai mē ontos nomou* (sin is not laid to account when there is no law [v. 13]). There men can live out their lives without having their ideals and errors disturbed. There their history can be interpreted as history of civilization and political history. We are not compelled to understand it in terms of God's grace and man's sin struggling against it, the facts do not force us to interpret it in these terms and these terms alone. There —and it is an open question whether it is for the good of those concerned or not—it is not revealed that man's history is the history of his broken covenant with God. There man's sin can always be concealed and extenuated and there are many evasions of the truth by which men escape only too successfully—not from the wrath of God, which is inescapable there and everywhere else—but from the knowledge of it, from the burning realization that the misery which men suffer is a punishment for their sins and so cannot be escaped at all. There men are not compelled to see the cleavage that runs through human existence and through all human achievements. There in all the triumphantly successful undertakings by which man tries to extricate himself from difficulties and help himself on in the great so-called progress of civilization and politics—there is proof that this cleavage has not been seen, that it has caused no real suffering, that, if the worst comes to the worst, there is always an escape from its reality in a little touch of tragedy which never fails to lead to the liberal toning down of the severity of the cleavage and to the comedy that it needs to help it through. Here a man can live, although here too he has sinned and here too he must die. That is how things stand where *hamartia oukh ellogeitai* (sin is not laid to account). That is what can and must happen where there is no Law. Here there can be no sinning *epi tō homoiōmati tēs parabaseōs Adam* (like Adam's transgression [v. 14]). Adam's sin is, indeed, repeated there but is not an open, explicit, conscious repetition of his rebellion against God. Where there is no election, there can be no sin committed in unfaithfulness to it. Where there is no calling, it cannot be slighted and disgraced. Where there is no sanctification, there is no desecration, no unsanctity. Where God has given no explicit commandment, there can be no high-handed transgression. Where there are no prophets, there can be no accusations and no threats. The sins of men outside Israel are, then, the same, and yet not the same, as the sin of Adam—the same because what Adam did, these men also do, but not the same, because these men are not confronted with God, as Adam was, and so act, not less badly, but in complete ignorance of the badness of what they do.

This situation gives rise to a problem with which Paul now has to deal. Does not the undeniable fact of the Law—of the special revelation of God's will in Israel—mean radical separation between the sin of Adam and the grace of Christ, and does it not destroy the relationship between them and invalidate the common ordering principle that they both share? Where God reveals Himself, the truth comes to light. God reveals Himself in the Law, and the truth that comes to light in this revelation is that the place where God reveals His covenant with man as the meaning of His will as Creator is the very place at which He and man fall so hopelessly apart. Where God's grace becomes so specially and explicitly great, where in the election and calling of Israel, in the mission of Moses, this extraordinary distinction is conferred upon man, just there the only result is a special *abounding—pleonazein* (v. 20)— of sin. There sin *ellogeitai* (is laid to account), its reality in human life is openly exposed and made unmistakably plain. Here we are dealing with the optimum of God's good will toward the creation. What more could be expected or desired of God than that He should turn toward men as He has turned toward Israel as its covenant Lawgiver and Lord? And here in Israel the only result is that it becomes obvious, as nowhere else, with what consistency (a thousand years of it!) man turns his back on Him, with what fruitless toil God stretches out His arms to a notoriously rebellious and perverse generation. Here God can have nothing to say to man but what He has said to him through the prophets of Israel in all their accusations and threats.

And if that is true of the green wood, what hope is there for the others, who have sinned like Israel, and still sin, but who have no part in Israel's distinction, in the great measure of grace that it received? What hope is there for the multitude of Gentiles in whose midst Israel was only an inconsiderable minority? Under these circumstances can we say that God's revelation achieved anything except the manifestation of His righteous wrath against men? In these circumstances, is it not the Gentiles who are fortunate, since they at least have had no such revelation, and have been spared the fearful knowledge and burdensome service of God that Israel had to bear? They can blindly dream their dreams; they can pursue their political conquests and their dreams; they can pursue their political conquests and their advances in civilization. They can go to meet the inevitable coming destruction unaware of what lies ahead, while Israel sees it coming and knows how dreadful it will be. But if that is so, it means that, although God's grace is present and effective in Israel in a unique way, His encounter with man in Israel only confirms what was already clear in Paradise, that man is neither capable nor worthy of the fellowship with God for which he was created, that he is radically separated from God's grace. Because of his guilt, there can be no positive relationship between him and God. Even the Law which came in to bind the two together can only be the final and impassable barrier that keeps them apart.

God exists and lives and is gracious, but man is without God, and against Him, and has fallen into a graceless existence, that can only end in his destruction. If that were all, the fifth chapter of Romans, and with it the whole New Testament, could never have been written—or could have been written only on the basis of an optimistic illusion whose very optimism would serve only to make it the more fearful. And when the revelation in the Law was completed in the appearance of the Messiah, did not Israel reject and crucify Him and so provide the final confirmation of all that it had done in its history to prove its alienation from the grace of God? If that were all, then the Old Testament promise of future grace would also be an illusion without any substance at all. For of what future grace could anything else be expected than that it should once more bring in its train the corresponding *pleonazein* (abounding) of human sin?

What has Paul to say to that? He first simply concedes the fact that the Law reveals man's sin, in v. 20*a*: *nomos de pareisēlthen hina pleonasē to paraptōma* (lit.: the law has slipped in in order that the transgression might abound). "The Law has come in between"—i.e., between Adam and Christ, between man and God, between sin and grace; it is in fact the great barrier between them—"that the transgression should become great"—not smaller, but great, greater than it is where there is no Law, no election, and no covenant, no calling and no grace, greater than anywhere else outside Israel, so great that it becomes objectively impossible not to recognize it, so great that in the life and destiny of the Jews it becomes a factor in world history, something that even the blindest and deafest Gentiles have to recognize and deal with, though in dealing with it they

85

misunderstand it by making it an excuse for anti-semitism, for hating the Jews. The Law has come in between so that the transgression is not covered up, but remains manifest—as manifest as the transgression of Adam. The remarkable proof of the existence of God which Frederick the Great's doctor is said to have offered to his loyal master is established for all time.[3]

The Holy Scriptures of Israel are an unambiguous proof of what happens when man opposes God. In comparison with this proof, all positive proofs of God's existence that Gentiles have produced in their ignorance or denial of God's revelation have no value at all. This is, of course, only a negative proof, but that is what makes it so genuine and so compelling. It is not a proof of man's devising, for it is based not on human thinking but on the factual witness of a part of human history to the revelation of God. In the history and destiny of the Jews, which takes place in the midst of world history, and yet is so different from the rest of world history that other nations have to recognize the uniqueness of it—in

---

[3] "Frederick the Great once asked his personal physician Zimmermann of Brugg in Aargau: 'Zimmermann, can you name me a single proof of the existence of God?' And Zimmermann replied, 'Your Majesty, the Jews!' "—Barth, *Dogmatics in Outline*, Eng. translation, p. 75.—TR.

that there is proof that the history of the world is not in the exclusive control of human thought and human achievement, but that in it there is at work a Will that is not man's will, One who is man's opponent in the game and whose moves are secret and impossible to control. The Jew who provides this proof of God provides at the same time proof of his own sin and his own fall.

The Jew is the *paraptōma* (transgression) that abounded. The only thing that his history can reveal is man's rebellion; the only thing that his destiny can reveal is man's misery. The antisemitic misunderstanding is natural and quite understandable. But that does not alter the fact that the mission of the Jews is to represent in themselves human rebellion and human suffering and so to provide in themselves the only genuine and convincing proof that man can provide of the existence of God. The sin of man and the guilt and punishment that follow it can *abound, pleonazein,* and can be revealed in the midst of human history: that is what happened in the Old Testament and in the subsequent history of Israel through the intervention of the Law. And that was what had to happen. That was why the Law had to intervene. The wound had to stay open or it could not be healed. Adam had to remain Adam or he could not be reconciled. That is what Paul concedes in the first sentence of v. 20—or, rather, that is the bold assertion that he, who is himself an Israelite, makes against the way in which his own people have misunderstood their election and calling, and against the antisemitic error which was not unknown even in his day. It was inevitable that God's chosen people, to whom He gave the Law, should achieve nothing but the final and absolute *pleonazein* (abounding) of the sinfulness of man.

That being so, what is left of the glory of the chosen people? There remains to it only the glory of God's grace, which it never deserved and to which it never responded by showing any faithfulness or constancy or gratitude that might have fulfilled the covenant between it and God. The only glory that remains to it is that, in spite of itself, it is and will be for all time the called and elected people of God. But what, on the other hand, is left of all the scorn and hate of the other nations against Israel? What advantage have they over the Jews, except that they are not Jews, and are not distinguished by God's special revelation of grace, and so are not exposed as what they are, so do not have to live under God's judgment or suffer under his wrath? They are not

Ahasver,[4] they have somewhere to call "home"; they are untroubled, while the Jew is always troubled, and so makes trouble for himself and his fellow men. How can their scorn and hate of the Jew be justified, when the Jew is only the bearer and exponent, the open sign, of the sinful life that they themselves are secretly living and of the hidden destiny that they will have to endure? The sin which becomes great in the existence of the Jew is their own sin, except that they, being less endowed with grace, are spared such an abounding of sin—sin is not revealed so clearly among them. Should they not be grateful to the Jews because they have borne the burden of God's grace alone and kept it from falling upon, and crushing, all other men?

But to see that, they would have to understand what Paul goes on to say in v. 20b: *hou de epleonasen hē hamartia, hypereperisseusen hē charis*— "Where sin became great, grace became much greater." Where that is not recognized, the Jew must go on stubbornly asserting his own superiority over the Gentiles, and the Gentile must go on despising the Jews. For without this further knowledge, neither can see that sin has become great through the inter-

---

[4] The Wandering Jew of the legend.—TR.

vention of the Law. Without this further knowledge, the Jew does not see it, because he persists in his rebellion against grace and cannot possibly let himself be convinced, even by his own Holy Scriptures and the whole experience of his history, that God's judgment pronounces him guilty of sin. And without this further knowledge, the non-Jew does not see it, because without the revelation of God's grace, he cannot possibly understand that Israel's sin is the exposure of the sin of all men, and that Israel's destiny is proof of the existence of God. Without the knowledge that grace became much greater at the place where sin became so great, Jew and non-Jew alike must remain blind to the truth about each other.

But what does it mean to say that grace became much greater at the very place where sin became great? From the whole context of the chapter, Paul must have been thinking here of one thing. The people of Israel, which is convicted by the Law of rebellion against God's grace, the people that has offered its covenant-Lord and Lawgiver nothing but unfaithfulness and disobedience, this stock that has been cut down right to the ground and has withered away, has been awakened to new life by a miraculous act of God in its midst, for from it there has sprung up the new shoot, Jesus Christ. Out of Israel comes the Christ who bears but also bears away the guilt of Israel and the guilt of all men in His death; He shows how serious that guilt is in the sight of God, but He also annuls it, and so is Himself the forgiveness of all the sins of the past and of the present; He is the *righteous* man. And out of Israel comes the Christ who, having endured the punishment and death of Israel and of all men, makes an end of death in His resurrection, so that it does not have to be endured any more, and so becomes Himself the pledge of deliverance from every trouble of the past and of the present; He is the *living* man. That is grace becoming much greater at the place where sin became so great. In Christ sin abounded but grace abounded even more.

Jesus Christ was a Jew. That is the fact which at one stroke makes nonsense of all Jewish pride and of all antisemitic scorn. Jesus Christ was a Jew and so He also was subjected to the Law. He also was set in the place where God's grace reveals man's sin. But there is more to it than that. He was the only one who completely and genuinely stood in that place; He was *the* Jew. There is no other Jew like Him because He alone of His own free will incorporated in His own person the man who rebels against God and has to bear God's wrath. There is a substitution of Israel for other peoples. But what is that compared with the substitution of Christ for Israel, beside His acceptance of the mission of the Jews? All other Jews have in the end only endured that mission, but He and He alone freely and of His own initiative took it upon Himself. Not only was Christ Israel, He chose to be Israel—and to be the Israel that was subject to the Law and that through the Law was accused and convicted of its sin. And just in that way He was Israel's Messiah, *the* Israelite, whose coming was the expectation and goal of all Israel's history. And yet He was a Messiah whom no Israelite father could beget as his son, for He could only be God's Son and as such had to be engrafted into Israel from the outside as the beginning of the new, true Israel of God. In this preeminent way He was a Jew. By freely submitting Himself to the Law He fulfilled it. And He submitted Himself to the Law in order that he might take upon Himself Israel's sin and Israel's punishment, and so the hidden sin and the secret condemnation that were revealed in Israel but that belonged to all men. He took that sin and that punishment upon Himself when He was pronounced guilty and put to death and because it was as Son of God that He bore them,

He took away the sin and the punishment from men. That is something no other Jew has done, that is something He has done and He alone. That is His work as the Jew *par excellence,* as "Jesus of Nazareth, the King of the Jews." That is how grace became so much greater in the very place where sin had become so great—where it had been clearly revealed as *homoiōma parabaseōs Adam* (like Adam's transgression).

But there is another side to v. 20 which must now be explained. Here the notorious rejection of Christ by the Jews can be seen in a new light. The appearing of Christ can and must certainly be understood as the last and perfect stage of God's revelation to Israel. Jesus Himself often ranged Himself with John the Baptist and all the prophets before him whom Israel rejected and put to death. Now once more God stretches out His hands, "Last of all he sent his son to them saying, 'They will respect my son' " (Matt. 21:37). So also the beginning of Hebrews: "By many tokens and in various ways God spoke of old to the fathers through the prophets, but on this last day he has spoken to us through the son whom he has appointed heir" (Heb. 1:1). It is quite true that the Jews laid violent hands upon this Son and Heir and so finally rejected their own Messiah.

Christ and Adam

It is quite true that when, with the appearing of Christ, grace abounded, Israel once again and finally showed itself to be the people in whom Adam's sin abounded. It is true that here at the end of its history it gave final proof of the opposition between God's will and man's will that had been the theme of all its history under the Law.

The implication that it is therefore accursed of God and the proper object of man's hate and scorn is for the same reason completely invalid and utterly unjustified. Nothing else could have happened. It was inevitable that the people of the revelation should once again confirm its opposition to God. The time when God sealed the covenant with Israel by Himself intervening on man's behalf and so made His grace to overflow, was bound to be the time when Israel finally disowned the covenant and proved itself absolutely unworthy of the grace of God. The whole dark story of the Old Testament is only the prelude to this final act of rebellion whereby Israel rejected its Messiah who had come in superabounding grace to reconcile it with God. But in thus rejecting Christ Israel acted as the representative of all other men. Here, as in its whole history, it has only done what every other people would also have done had it received the same revelation of

God's grace. And all this was inevitable because it was only by rejecting Christ that Israel could serve the gracious purposes of God. If grace was to abound, if sin and death were to be removed from the world, Christ *had* to be condemned as a sinner and *had* to die. If God was to show mercy to man by saving him from sin and death, and if at the same time He was to honor His own righteousness as man's Creator and Lord, He *had* to intervene on man's behalf, He had to come to man's rescue and let Himself be condemned as a sinner and put to death on the cross. That was what happened in Jesus Christ and that is how in Him grace became greater than sin. God did not rest content with making known His will in the Law, but in and with the Law He made known His promise that was greater than the Law, His promise to intervene on behalf of the men who had sinned against Him and made themselves liable to suffering and death. And that divine intervention is the *hyperperisseuein* ("superabounding") of the grace of God.

For a thousand years Israel sinned, but for a thousand years God was faithful, so that the Old Testament is not just the dark prelude to Israel's rejection of its Messiah; it is also the witness of God's promise to be gracious, and so it is the prelude to God's act of intervention in which He takes upon Himself the open shame of Israel and the secret shame of all men. That is why the Old Testament can without any illusion look forward to the promised grace of God. God does not rest content with demanding from man faithful allegiance to the covenant He has made. For man is unfaithful and his response to the covenant is to crucify Christ and to give final proof that he deserves nothing but the wrath of God. But in His Son God provides this human faithfulness that man has failed to provide. And so the human faithfulness of the man Jesus is the *hyperperisseuein* of the grace of God. But to show this faithfulness God's Son must take man's place and bear man's shame and suffer man's death. It is God's will that that shame should be removed. But no other than He Himself is able to remove it. God does not will the death of the sinner, but rather that he should be converted and live. But that he should be converted and live can only be God's work, and so to complete that work God Himself takes man's place as a sinner who is condemned to die. And so the Jews, when they condemned Christ to a sinner's death, were in fact carrying out the good, righteous and merciful will of God. They did it as completely unworthy and completely blameworthy instruments. In doing it they showed once again and finally that they themselves and man in general, for whom in their way they were substitutes, were transgressors who fully deserved to be condemned. But they did it. The *pleonazein* (abounding) of sin was indispensable if the *hyperperisseuein* ("superabounding") of grace was to follow. And this indispensable condition was fulfilled when the Jews handed over Christ to a sinner's death.

When God came to reconcile man, man's response was no act of good will stimulated by *gratia praeveniens* (prevenient grace) and co-operating with it on the basis of a still intact *liberum arbitrium* (free will): it was on the contrary this *pleonazein* of sin. And that was what man had to do here, if God was really to let Himself be covered in human shame, so that He could destroy it and win the victory over it for the sake of His own righteousness and the salvation of men. Here clearly man had to act and co-operate and he did act and co-operate when Israel rejected Christ and thus brought its transgressions to their full measure. That was of course the act of a people who stood under the curse of God, and that was hateful and despicable in the highest degree. But there is something else we must now add to that. Through this act of this people God has taken their curse upon Himself in His Son and so has Himself become hateful and despicable on their behalf and in their stead. If this people had not acted in this way, the Son of God would not have borne the curse of sin and the hatefulness and shame of men.

The accusation against the Jews over their rejection of Christ is in the last resort invalid because either it is completely null and void or it falls upon God Himself. In doing as they did they were acquitted from the guilt and punishment that their action deserved by God's action in bearing their guilt and punishment on their behalf. If they had not acted as they did, God would not have borne their guilt and punishment and they would not have been acquitted at all. For what they did to Christ the Jews cannot be excused, but neither can they be accused or condemned. "Who will bring any accusation against God's elect?" cried Paul the Jew in a later passage, and there he was certainly thinking also of his own people, God's chosen people, who were *par excellence* the sinners who deserved death. "It is God that justifies them. Who will condemn them? It is Christ that died, nay rather who has been raised up, who is at the right hand of God, who makes intercession for us" (Rom. 8:33-34). The death and resurrection of Christ make nonsense of Jewish pride, but they also take every possible justification for antisemitism away. It is possible to be pro-Jewish, and it is possible to be anti-Jewish, only when for some reason men are not aware how through the act of the Jews God took upon Himself man's guilt and shame, how the Jews were the instruments of the *hyperperisseuein* ("superabounding") of God's grace amidst the *pleonazein* (abounding) of the sin of man. When we are aware of that, the only relevant way of understanding the relationship of Jews and non-Jews is the way Paul himself understands it in Rom. 9-11.

But v. 20 still needs to be interpreted in yet a third way. When Paul spoke of the *pleonazein* or *hyperperisseuein* of grace, he always thought not only of God's grace breaking through into the world of sin and death in the death and resurrection of Christ; he always thought also of the breaking down of that middle wall of partition which had limited God's revelation to Israel only and prevented it from being made known to all men. He thought, in fact, of the outpouring of the Holy Spirit upon all flesh. The death and resurrection of Jesus Christ mean that God has now ceased to be the God only of the Jews, and has openly revealed Himself as the God of the Gentiles and so of all men. He has now ceased to be

God only inside Israel, and has become God outside Israel as well, and both outside and inside He is the same. Here also all barriers have been broken down—taken away. The covenant was secretly from the beginning a covenant with all men, and it has now been revealed as such through the outpouring of the Holy Ghost.

God's grace was and is not for one people only but for all men. When Israel received that revelation it received it not for itself only but that it might hold it in trust for all other peoples. And so the sin that has been revealed in Israel's history and in Israel's rejection of Christ is not only its own sin but the sin of all men. And when God in Christ bore the shame of Israel, that gracious intervention was not only on behalf of Israel but on behalf of all men. And so the *hyperperisseuein* of God's grace means not just the reconciliation of the Jews but the reconciliation of the Gentiles too. But where is the link here? How do the Gentiles come in? The *pleonazein* of man's sin seems at first sight to be entirely the work of the Jews, seems indeed to be their conflict with their Messiah. How then can the *hyperperisseuein* of grace become something that affects all men? The answer is given in the Passion narratives of the Gospels. All of them emphasize that the crucifixion of

Christ and Adam

Christ is not directly the work of the Jews, but that, while it is certainly instigated by the Jews, its execution is the work of the Roman Governor, Pontius Pilate, and his subordinates, and so the work of the Gentiles. The Jews "handed over" Jesus to be crucified—that is the technical term used by the New Testament to describe the part played by the Jews. Their sin became great in that they expelled Jesus from the sphere of the holy people and gave him up to the unclean Gentiles outside. And it was at the hands of these unclean Gentiles, who were not elected and not called, at the hands of those who, according to Eph. 2:12, "were without God in the world," that He was hung on the gallows—not inside Jerusalem, but outside the city gates. And in that highly significant way He came for the first time to the Gentiles. And because that was the way He came, they also had a part in the *pleonazein* of Israel's transgression as the executioners of the Jewish Messiah. And like the Jews they also had a part that did not call for any positive co-operation or good will. By the way they acted, they made it obvious that they were no better than the Jews.

Since Cain's murder of Abel the flagrant sins and the notorious outrages of world history had always been the responsibility of Gentiles rather than Jews.

More was required of the Jews than of the Gentiles, but if we could forget this greater requirement, we might, in retrospect, wonder whether the accusations and threats of the prophets might not have been more justly aimed at the Gentiles, whose sins were often worse than the sins of the Jews. But however that may be, and however one apportions the guilt for Jesus' death between Jews and Gentiles, it is still true that in the condemnation and execution of Jesus the Gentiles are actively involved. And the part they play there shows that they are the flagrant sinners, the direct murderers of Christ. The first Gentile who has dealings with God's Son is called Pilate. He pronounces the judgment by which Jesus is made a sinner and by which He has to die. He orders the execution of that judgment. He sets the watch on Christ's grave. He is responsible for completing the act which the Jews are equally responsible for beginning. Is then his handwashing only hypocritical and useless? Perhaps it is not as simple as that. The saying of Luke 23:34—"Father, forgive them, for they know not what they do"—refers in its context not to the Jews, who first re-emerge from the background later, but to the Gentiles who have carried out the actual crucifixion. It is indeed applicable only to them for they are the men whom Paul describes in vv. 13-14, the men who sinned without the Law and so were not convicted of their sin, who in their ignorance did not know that they were sinning against God. They did not, in fact, know what they were doing. And it is for them that Christ now prays that what they have done may be forgiven them.

Does that mean that Christ died for these Gentiles and for the sin that abounded in them? Does that mean that He has taken sin and death away from them as well as from the Jews? That was what Paul believed and what the whole New Testament believes. That was what was revealed to the Apostles on the day of Pentecost. There are several good reasons why Pilate's name should have a place in the Creed. One of them is that he was the Gentile who received Jesus from the hands of the Jews. When He came to be judged and executed by Pilate, Jesus, the Jewish Messiah, became the Saviour of the world, and could later be proclaimed as such in the missionary preaching of the Apostles. What was done there was certainly not an act of good will on the part of the heathen world. On the contrary: in Pilate's encounter with Jesus, the Gentiles at the eleventh hour recapitulated in themselves the whole history of Israel, made in due form common cause with the Jews against God, and so came to share Israel's curse and hatefulness and shame.

At the very last moment before the door was closed, the non-Jews in the person of Pilate managed to enter into the very heart of the revelation in the Law, as it was on the point of reaching its goal and its end. This happened that they might in due form have a share in the *pleonazein* (abounding) of the transgression, and might show beyond all doubt that they are no better and no worse than the Jews (vv. 13-14). They are also the instruments by which God accomplished his righteous and merciful will for the salvation of men. They now cease to be mere spectators and become fellow workers in this critical event. They also co-operate as sinners—how could it be otherwise?—and so they also are included in God's gracious purpose in this event, the reconciliation of the world with Himself. This is not merely a religious reconciliation, but, in all seriousness, the reconciliation of the world, for the Passion narratives make it clear how, through Jesus, Pilate and Herod were reconciled, and Pilate and the Jewish churchmen worked hand in glove once more. From now on, even the Gentiles who have no Law are without excuse, but, from now on, there is no accusation or condemnation against them because the death and resurrection of the Saviour of the world have taken their guilt and their condemnation away. For now they have openly shared in the *pleonazein* of the transgression. "But where the transgression became great, just there grace has become very much greater." And so they also have a share in the *hyperperisseuein* ("superabounding") of grace.

God is now revealed not only as the God of the Jews but also as the God of the Gentiles. Pontius Pilate certainly does belong in the Creed. The outpouring of the Holy Spirit upon all flesh became objectively possible through what this Pontius Pilate did with his guilty-innocent hands. He who suffered, at the hands of unclean Gentiles, died and rose again, for unclean Gentiles, as well as for clean Jews, that they might be reconciled to God. He is the Advocate for all flesh. It is not the missionary preaching of the Apostles that first makes Him Saviour of the world. That preaching can only witness to One who has already died at the hands of both Jews and Gentiles and has in His resurrection revealed the whole world's reconciliation to God.

What have we learned from vv. 13-14 and 20? They have shown us that between the sin of Adam and the grace of Christ there is a barrier which man is unable to cross. But God has espoused man's cause. He has done that by electing Israel and giving it His Law. He has done it by causing His own Son to become man as an Israelite and by making Him subject to the Law. But man, confronted with this act of God, has revealed that both as Jew and as Gentile, he is in rebellion against God. When God embraced man's cause in this special and unique way, man's reaction proved conclusively that he was still the Adam he had been from the beginning. He is not willing to cross the barrier that divides sin from grace. His contribution is only the rejection and crucifixion of the Messiah of Israel, who is also the Saviour of the world. But God has crossed this barrier. Where man has refused, God has not refused. He Himself has come to the rescue of the men who refused. He has done well what man has done ill. That is the secret of His revelation in the Law in Israel. That is the secret of the closing and completion of that revelation in Jesus Christ. God takes man's transgression seriously by taking it upon Himself: He Himself becomes the sinner and dies in man's place and so makes both sin and death pass away. Adam and Christ are thus distinguished from each other. The history of Israel under the Law shows that there is no way from the sin of Adam to the grace of Christ, but that there is a way from the grace of Christ to the sin of Adam. The Law excludes Adam from the grace of Christ, but by fulfilling the Law Christ can take upon Himself Adam's sin. Adam excludes Christ: but Christ includes Adam. Adam does not become Christ, but Christ, without ceasing to be Christ, and indeed just because He is Christ, becomes Adam as well. And because Christ thus identifies Himself with Adam's sin and Adam's death, Adam the sinner becomes a witness to Christ, the Reconciler, *typos tou mellontos* (a type of the one to come [v. 14]). That is what we learn about the relationship between Christ and Adam from the Law that stands midway between them. And so to take the Law into account is not to retract what is said in the rest of Rom. 5 about the superiority and priority of the grace of Christ over the sin of Adam. To know what the Law means is rather the strongest, and, for Paul, the decisive proof that Adam is subordinate to Christ, and that our relationship to Adam is less essential than our relationship to Christ.

Jesus Christ is the secret truth about the essential nature of man, and even sinful man is still essentially related to Him. That is what we have learned from Rom. 5:12-21.

Now we shall try to summarize our conclusions: We have seen how, according to vv. 1-11, Jesus Christ is a sharply-defined individual, and how, as such, He is clearly the representative of an undetermined multitude of other men. In His life and destiny He represents and anticipates their life and their destiny so that they, without ceasing to be distinct individuals, must make their life an image and reflection of His life and must work out the destiny that overtook them in Him. They have to identify themselves with Him, because He has already identified Himself with them. There is no question of any merging or any confusion between Him and them, but neither can there be any question of any abstraction or separation. He in His individuality is theirs, and so they in their individuality can only be His. The ineffaceable distinction between Him and them is the guarantee of their indissoluble unity with Him. They as receivers are subordinated and yet indissolubly related to Him as Giver; they as members are subordinated and yet indissolubly united to Him as Head.

But vv. 1-11 only speak of Jesus Christ and those who *believe* in Him. If we read that first part of the chapter by itself, we might quite easily come to the conclusion that for Paul Christ's manhood is significant only for those who are united to Him in faith. We would then have no right to draw any conclusion about the relationship between Christ and *man as such,* from what Paul says about the "religious" relationship between Christ and Christians. We could not then expect to find in the manhood of Christ the key to the essential nature of man.

But in vv. 12-21 Paul does not limit his context to Christ's relationship to believers but gives fundamentally the same account of His relationship to all men. The context is widened from Church history to world history, from Christ's relationship to Christians to His relationship to all men. It should be noted that in these verses there is no further mention of faith or even of the gift of the Holy Spirit, and that the first person plural which is continually used in vv. 1-11 is here (with the exception of the last phrase of v. 21) replaced by a quite general third person plural. What is said here applies generally and universally, and not merely to one limited group of men. Here "religious" presuppositions are not once hinted at. The fact of Christ is here presented as something that dominates and includes all men. The nature of Christ objectively conditions human nature and the work of Christ makes an objective difference to the life and destiny of all men. Through Christ grace overflows upon them, bringing them pardon and justification and opening before them a prospect of life with God. In short, "grace rules," as it is put in v. 21. And all that is in exact correspondence to what happens to human nature in its objective relationship to Adam. There sin rules, in exactly the same way, and all men become sinners and unrighteous in Adam, and as such must die. The question about what is the special mark of the *Christian* is just not raised at all. What we are told is what it means for man as such that his objective relationship to Adam is subordinate to and dependent upon and included in his objective relationship to Christ. The question raised here—as distinct from vv. 1-11—concerns the relationship between Christ and all men.

Paul had obviously no intention of fathering an idle and arbitrary speculation when in this passage he passed on to this further account of the same subject. If we have understood the *dia touto* (therefore) of v. 12 rightly, his intention was rather to consolidate the special account he had already given of the relationship between Christ and faith, by placing it in this wider and more general context. Our standing as believers is as vv. 1-11 have described it, because our standing as men is as vv. 12-21 describe it. Our relationship to Christ as believers is based upon our prior relationship to Him as Adam's children and heirs. For even when we were, in the words of vv. 1-11, weak, sinners, godless, and enemies, Christ died for us and so brought us into His Kingdom and under His power.

We have come *to* Christ as believers and Christians, because we had already come *from* Christ, so that there was nothing else for us to do but believe in Him. What is said in vv. 1-11 is not just "religious" truth that only applies to specially talented, specially qualified, or specially guided men; it is truth for *all* men, whether they know it or not, as surely as they are all Adam's children and heirs. The assurance of Christians, as it is described in vv. 1-11, has as its basis the fact that the Christian sphere is not limited to the "religious" sphere. What is *Christian* is secretly but fundamentally identical with what is *universally human.* Nothing in true human nature can ever be alien or irrelevant to the Christian; nothing in true human nature can ever attack or surpass or annul the objective reality of the Christian's union with Christ. Much in true human nature is unrelated to "religion," but nothing in true human nature is unrelated to the Christian faith. That means that we can understand true human nature only in the light of the Christian gospel that we believe. For Christ stands above and is first, and Adam stands below and is second. So it is Christ that reveals the true nature of man. Man's nature in Adam is not, as is usually assumed, his true and original nature; it is only truly human at all in so far as it reflects and corresponds to essential human nature as it is found in Christ. True human nature, therefore, can only be understood by Christians who look to Christ to discover the essential nature of man. Vv. 12-21 are revolutionary in their insistence that what is true of Christians must also be true of all men. That is a principle that has an incalculable significance for all our action and thought. To reject this passage as empty speculation is tantamount to denying that the human nature of Christ is the final revelation of the true nature of man.

What Rom. 5:12-21 is specially concerned to make clear is that man as we know him, man in Adam who sins and dies, has his life so ordered that he is both a distinct individual and, at the same time, the responsible representative of humanity and of all other men. In the same way there are no other responsible representatives of humanity than individual men. We are what Adam was and so are all our fellow men. And the one Adam is what we and all men are. Man is at once an individual and only an individual, and, at the same time, without in any way losing his individuality, he is the responsible representative of all men. He is always for himself and always for all men. That being so, can we build on this foundation? Is it true that essential human nature must always be the existence of the man in humanity and of humanity in the man? We recognize that, first, only in relation to Adam and the many who are like him, and so only in relation to sinful and dying men like ourselves. But have we understood man correctly when we understand him in that way? Could not all that be quite wrong? Might not humanity be a corporate personality of which individuals are only insignificant manifestations or fragmentary parts? Or might not the whole notion of humanity be a fiction, and the reality consist only of a collection of individuals each essentially unrelated to the others and each responsible only for himself? Rom. 5:12-21 points in neither of these directions. If we base our thinking on this passage, we can have nothing to do with either collectivism on the one hand or individualism on the other. It understands the true man in neither of these ways.

But how does this passage come to be so definite about its own interpretation of the true man? For it is dealing expressly with Adam and so with corrupt man, and it might seem questionable to base such definite statements about the true nature of man upon our knowledge of him. What is Paul's authority for basing a categorical conclusion about the structure of human nature upon nothing sounder than his knowledge of fallen man? We have seen that Paul dares to draw this conclusion because he sees Adam not in isolation but in his relationship to Christ. And for him Christ and Adam do not represent two conflicting interpretations of human nature. For in that case the doubt as to which was ultimately valid would still arise—and the tone of vv. 1-11 shows that Paul has no doubts at all. The answer is in vv. 13-14 and 20, where it is shown that the formal correspondence and identity between Adam and Christ is based upon their material disparity. In the encounter between them Christ has more right and power, and Adam less. It is only in this disparity of status and in this disproportion that they can be compared. Adam is subordinate to Christ, and not Christ to Adam. And if Adam is subordinate to Christ, then Adam represents true and genuine human nature in so far as he shows us the man in humanity and humanity in the man. Whatever else in his representation of human nature may have to be accounted for by its later corruption and ruin, this ordering principle at least belongs to its condition and character as created and untouched by sin. For the subordinate representation of human nature in Adam here corresponds to its primary representation in Christ. In Christ also, the man is in humanity and humanity is in the man. With one important difference: Adam is not God's Son become man, and so he cannot, like Him, be man, and at the same time be *over* all men. Adam, as the one, can represent the many; he as man can represent humanity— but only as one among others. Thus he can represent all the others only in the same way that each of them can represent him. Adam has no essential priority of status over other men. He cannot be their lord and head; he cannot determine their life and their destiny. He can anticipate their life and destiny in himself, only in so far as he is the first man among many others, only in so far as he is *primus inter pares*. The *pollō mallon* (much more) of vv. 15-17 marks this difference. Where it is taken into account, what remains of the identity between Adam and Christ is the unity of the one and the many on both sides, of his deeds and their deeds, of his condition and theirs. In this unity Christ is, like Adam, man. In this unity of the one and the many Adam is the type and likeness of Christ, although formally he differs from Christ because he is not lord and head in this unity, and materially he differs from Him, because his nature is perverted by sin. But this unity, as such, belongs not to the perversion of his nature but to its original constitution. And so Paul makes no arbitrary assertion, and he is not deceiving himself when he presupposes this unity as simply given even in Adam. He does so because he has found it given first and primarily in Christ.

Christ is not only God's Son; He is also a man who is not a sinner like Adam and all of us. He is true man in an absolute sense, and it is in His humanity that we have to recognize true human nature in the condition and character in which it was willed and created by God. To it there certainly belongs this unity of man and humanity. When we inquire about the true nature of man and seek an answer in terms of this unity, we are on firm ground, in so far as even sinful man, whom alone we know, reflects back, as far as this unity is concerned, the human nature of Christ and so has not ceased to be true man and has not ceased to show man's true nature to us.

INDEX

Index

Adam: formal resemblance
to Christ, 42-48, 63; individuality and humanity of,
112 f.; and Israel, 76 f.;
material subordination to
Christ, 44-51, 55, 64 f.,
74, 105 f., 112 f.; as
"type" of Christ, 9 f., 39 f.,
46 f., 74 f., 107 f., 116;
and world history, 18; *see
also*, Man, Sin
Anthropology; *see* Man,
Doctrine of
Antisemitism, 86, 88 f., 90 f.,
98 f.
Atonement, Doctrine of, 8
Augustine, 7, 10

Christ: faithfulness of, 95 f.;
and formal resemblance to
Adam, 41-48, 63; humilia-
tion of, 67, 97 f.; individuality of, 34 ff.; Kingdom
of, 37 f., 111; material superiority, to Adam, 19 f.,
37 f., 43-49, 58 ff., 64, 74,
105 f., 114 f.; representative humanity of, 11, 18 f.,
34, 42, 47, 75, 107, 114 ff.;
universality of, 10, 45, 99-
105; *see also* Death; Man;
Resurrection
Christians, 45, 108-12
Christology, as basis of theology, 14 f.
Church Dogmatics, 9, 9 n.,
13-16, 17
Condemnation, 51-54, 70
Covenant, the, 76-79, 94 f.

Death: of Christ, 31, 34, 58-
63, 65-72, 96, 100 f.; lordship of, 48, 53-57, 70 f.,
78 f.; as penalty of sin, 7,
10 f., 49

121

Index

Easter, 68 f.
Election, 16
Enoch, Books of, 13
Exegesis, method of, 8 f., 11 f.

Frederick the Great, 86

Gentiles: ignorance of, 79-82, 102; reconciled by Christ, 103 ff.; rejection of Christ by, 100 ff.
Grace: of Christ, 58 f., 71 f.; to Israel, 82 f., 88 f.; lordship of, 44, 48; power of, over sin, 50-58, 89-97, 105 f.; result of, 50-58; theology of, 7

History: of Israel, 76 f., 86 f., 91 f., 94; world, 18 f., 40, 79 f.; 101
Hope, 30, 55, 65

Israel, 54, 75 f.; glory of, 88; and Adam, 76 f.; as representative of human sin, 87 ff., 94, 100; revelation to, 79, 82 f.

Jews: as proof of existence of God, 86 f.; rejection of Christ by, 93-99

Judgment, 51, 54, 59
Justification, 29-32

Law: fulfilled by Christ, 90-93; as revelation of sin, 85, 105 f.
Life, as gift of grace, 54 f., 60, 65, 70
Love, of God, 30 f.

Man: doctrine of, 8, 15 f., 36 ff.; relationship of, to Adam, 17 f., 37-48, 109-16; relationship of, to Christ, 15 f., 34-45, 55-64, 69 f., 72-75, 107 f., 114-17

Natural theology, 15 f.
New Testament, 13, 84

Old Testament, 70, 76 f., 84 f.
One and Many, 42, 49, 62, 70, 72-75
Original sin, 7, 10, 13, 18 f.

Pardon, 51 f., 53, 55, 62 f.
Philo of Alexandria, 13
Pontius Pilate, 101-05

Reconciliation, 30, 32-34, 58-62, 65 f., 104 f.

122

Index

Reformation, 7
Resurrection, 32 ff., 58-60, 65-73
Righteous Decision of God, 30-32, 34 f., 41, 54 f.
Roman Catholicism, 7, 14

Salvation, 30-33, 58 f., 65
Sin: of Adam, 7, 10 f., 18 f., 40, 49 f., 58 f., 68 f., 81; of Gentiles, 79-82, 100 ff.; of Israel, 76-88; mystery of, 65 f., 71 f.; original, 7, 10, 13, 18 f.; results of, 50-58, 69

Thomism, 14
Truth, in Christ and in Adam, 50, 57-62, 65, 70-74

Vulgate, the, 7 f.

Wisdom of Solomon, 13
Word of God, 13 ff., 18 f.
Wrath of God, 69, 80, 83

CPSIA information can be obtained
at www.ICGtesting.com
Printed in the USA
BVHW08s0845041018
529173BV00002B/423/P